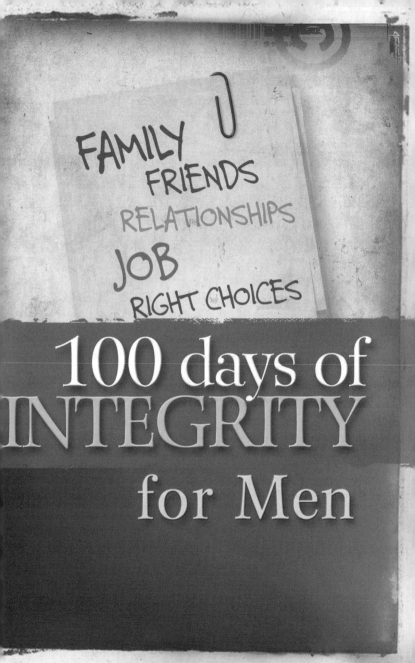

FAMILY
FRIENDS
RELATIONSHIPS
JOB
RIGHT CHOICES

100 days of INTEGRITY

for Men

The quoted ideas expressed in this book (but not Scripture verses) are not, in all cases, exact quotations, as some have been edited for clarity and brevity. In all cases, the author has attempted to maintain the speaker's original intent. In some cases, quoted material for this book was obtained from secondary sources, primarily print media. While every effort was made to ensure the accuracy of these sources, the accuracy cannot be guaranteed. For additions, deletions, corrections, or clarifications in future editions of this text, please write Freeman-Smith, LLC.

The Holy Bible, King James Version

The Holy Bible, New King James Version (NKJV) Copyright © 1982 by Thomas Nelson, Inc. Used by permission.

New Century Version®. (NCV) Copyright © 1987, 1988, 1991 by Word Publishing, a division of Thomas Nelson, Inc. All rights reserved. Used by permission.

The Holman Christian Standard Bible™ (Holman CSB) Copyright © 1999, 2000, 2001 by Holman Bible Publishers. Used by permission.

The Holy Bible, New International Version®. (NIV) Copyright © 1973, 1978, 1984 International Bible Society. Used by permission of Zondervan. All rights reserved.

The Holy Bible. New Living Translation (NLT) copyright © 1996 Tyndale Charitable Trust. Used by permission of Tyndale House Publishers.

The New American Standard Bible®, (NASB) Copyright © 1960, 1962, 1963, 1968, 1971, 1972, 1973, 1975, 1977, 1995 by The Lockman Foundation. Used by permission.

Scripture taken from The Message. (MSG) Copyright © 1993, 1994, 1995, 1996, 2000, 2001, 2002. Used by permission of NavPress Publishing Group.

Cover Design by Kim Russell / Wahoo Designs
Page Layout by Bart Dawson

ISBN 978-1-60587-114-1

Printed in the United States of America

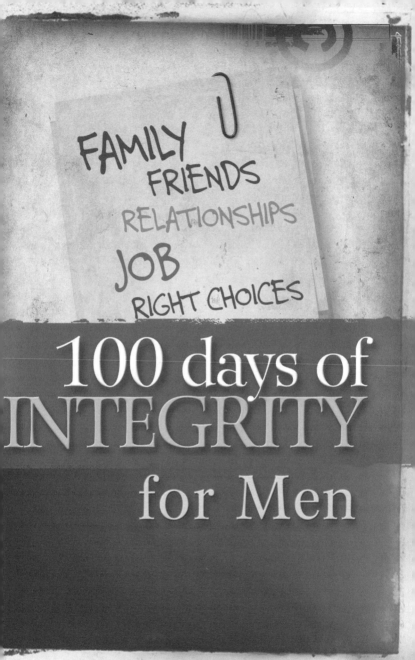

INTRODUCTION

Sometimes it seems that life here in the 21st century has been designed with an overriding purpose in mind: to test—and if possible, to tear down—your character. At almost every turn, you are tempted to take shortcuts, to follow the wrong role models, and to betray your conscience. If you fall prey to these temptations, you will inevitably disappoint your family, your community, and yourself. A far better strategy, of course, is to guard your integrity like you guard your wallet, and this book is intended to help.

This text contains 100 devotional readings that are intended to remind you, a Christian man, of the importance of integrity: keeping it, building it, and passing it on to the next generation. So, for the next 100 days, do yourself and your loved ones a big-league favor: read a chapter a day and internalize the ideas that you find here.

This text contains Biblically-based prescriptions for the inevitable challenges that accompany life-here-on-earth. As you consider your own circumstances, remember this: whatever the size of your challenge, whatever the scope of your temptation or your problem, God is bigger. Much bigger. He will instruct you, protect you, energize you, and heal you if you let Him. So let Him. Pray fervently, listen carefully, work diligently, and treat every single day as an exercise in character-building, because that's precisely what every day can be . . . and should be.

DAY 1

100 DAYS OF INTEGRITY

Blessed is the man who walks not in the counsel
of the ungodly, nor stands in the path of sinners, nor sits in
the seat of the scornful; but his delight is in the law of the
Lord, and in His law he meditates day and night. He shall be
like a tree planted by the rivers of water, that brings forth its
fruit in its season, whose leaf also shall not wither;
and whatever he does shall prosper.
Psalm 1:1-3 NKJV

You're about to begin a 100-day journey, an exploration of your character: what it is at this moment, what it should be today, and what it can become tomorrow. During the next 100 days, you will be challenged to examine your habits, your thoughts, your priorities, and your behaviors. And you'll be challenged to consider proven formulas for character-building, strategies for making the most of the talents and the opportunities that have been given to you by your Creator.

Billy Graham correctly observed, "Integrity is the glue that holds our way of life together. We must constantly strive to keep our integrity intact. When wealth is lost, nothing is lost; when health is lost, something is lost;

when character is lost, all is lost." Yet all too often, we find it far more convenient to be dishonest with ourselves, with our loved ones, and with our Father in heaven. And the results can be heartbreaking.

As Christians we are called to walk with God and to obey His commandments. But, we live in a world that presents us with countless temptations to wander far from God's path. These temptations have the potential to destroy us, in part, because they cause us to be dishonest with ourselves and with others.

Dishonesty is a habit. Once we start bending the truth, we're likely to keep bending it. A far better strategy, of course, is to acquire the habit of being completely forthright with God, with other people, and with ourselves.

Honesty, like its counterpart, is also a habit, a habit that pays powerful dividends for those who place character above convenience. So, for the next 100 days, make this simple promise to yourself and keep it: when you're tempted to bend the truth, even slightly—or to break it—ask yourself this question: "What does God want me to do?" Then listen carefully to your conscience. When you do, your actions will be honorable, and your character will take care of itself.

Before God changes our circumstances, He wants to change our hearts.

Warren Wiersbe

Maintaining your integrity in a world of sham is no small accomplishment.

Wayne Oates

Every time you refuse to face up to life and its problems, you weaken your character.

E. Stanley Jones

No man can use his Bible with power unless he has the character of Jesus in his heart.

Alan Redpath

TODAY'S INTEGRITY BUILDER

Take time to think about your own character, both your strong points and your weaknesses. Then list three aspects of your character—longstanding habits or troublesome behaviors—that you would like to modify during the next 100 days. Finally, ask God to be your partner as you take steps to improve yourself and your life.

The one who lives with integrity lives securely, but whoever perverts his ways will be found out.

Proverbs 10:9 Holman CSB

In all things showing yourself to be a pattern of good works; in doctrine showing integrity, reverence, incorruptibility . . . .

Titus 2:7 NKJV

Lead a quiet and peaceable life in all godliness and honesty.

1 Timothy 2:2 KJV

We also rejoice in our afflictions, because we know that affliction produces endurance, endurance produces proven character, and proven character produces hope.

Romans 5:3-4 Holman CSB

TODAY'S PRAYER

Dear Lord, every day can be an exercise in character-building, and that's what I intend to make this day. I will be mindful that my thoughts and actions have great consequences, consequences in my own life and in the lives of my loved ones. I will strive to make my thoughts and actions pleasing to You, so that I may be an instrument of Your peace, today and every day. Amen

DAY 2

BUILDING CHARACTER BY PUTTING GOD FIRST

But seek first the kingdom of God and His righteousness,
and all these things will be provided for you.

Matthew 6:33 Holman CSB

One of the quickest ways to build character—perhaps the only way—is to do it with God as your partner. So here's a question worth thinking about: Have you made God your top priority by offering Him your heart, your soul, your talents, and your time? Or are you in the habit of giving God little more than a few hours on Sunday morning? The answer to these questions will determine, to a surprising extent, the direction of your day and the condition of your character.

As you contemplate your own relationship with God, remember this: all of mankind is engaged in the practice of worship. Some folks choose to worship God and, as a result, reap the joy that He intends for His children to experience. Other folks, folks who are stubbornly determined to do it "their way," distance themselves from God by worshiping such things as earthly possessions or personal gratification. . . . and when they do, they suffer.

In the book of Exodus, God warns that we should place no gods before Him (v. 20:3). Yet all too often, we place our Lord in second, third, or fourth place as we worship the gods of pride, greed, power, or lust.

Does God rule your heart? Make certain that the honest answer to this question is a resounding yes. If you sincerely wish to build your character and your life on an unshakeable foundation, you must put your Creator in first place. No exceptions.

To God be the glory, great things He has done;
So loved He the world that He gave us His Son.

—

Fanny Crosby

We become whatever we are committed to.

Rick Warren

God calls us to be committed to Him, to be committed to making a difference, and to be committed to reconciliation.

Bill Hybels

God deserves first place in your life . . . and you deserve the experience of putting Him there.

Criswell Freeman

When all else is gone, God is still left. Nothing changes Him.

Hannah Whitall Smith

One with God is a majority.

Billy Graham

TODAY'S INTEGRITY BUILDER

Think about your priorities. Are you really putting God first in your life, or are you putting other things—things like possessions, pleasures, or personal status—ahead of your relationship with the Father? And if your priorities for life are misaligned, think of at least three things you can do today to put God where He belongs: in first place.

No one has ever seen God. If we love one another, God remains in us and His love is perfected in us.

1 John 4:12 Holman CSB

He that loveth not, knoweth not God; for God is love.

1 John 4:8 KJV

You shall have no other gods before Me.

Exodus 20:3 NKJV

Yet Lord, You are our Father; we are the clay, and You are our potter; we all are the work of Your hands.

Isaiah 64:8 Holman CSB

TODAY'S PRAYER

Dear Lord, today I will honor You with my thoughts, my actions, and my prayers. I will seek to please You, and I will strive to serve You. Your blessings are as limitless as Your love. And because I have been so richly blessed, I will worship You, Father, with thanksgiving in my heart and praise on my lips, this day and forever. Amen

DAY 3

PRAYER BUILDS CHARACTER

And everything—whatever you ask in prayer,
believing—you will receive.
Matthew 21:22 Holman CSB

In the battle to build character, prayer is an indispensable weapon. Your life is not a destination; it is a journey that unfolds day by day. And, that's exactly how often you should seek direction from your Creator: one day at a time, each day followed by the next, without exception.

Daily prayer and meditation is a matter of will and habit. You must willingly organize your time by carving out quiet moments with God, and you must form the habit of daily worship. When you do, you'll discover that no time is more precious than the silent moments you spend with your Heavenly Father.

God promises that the prayers of righteous men can accomplish great things. God promises that He answers prayer (although His answers are not always in accordance with our desires). God invites us to be still and to feel His presence. So pray. Start praying before the sun comes up and keep praying until you fall off to sleep at night. Pray about matters great and small; and be watchful for the answers that God most assuredly sends your way.

Is prayer an integral part of your daily life or is it a hit-or-miss routine? Do you "pray without ceasing," or is your prayer life an afterthought? Do you regularly pray in the solitude of the early morning darkness, or do you bow your head only when others are watching?

The quality of your spiritual life will be in direct proportion to the quality of your prayer life. Prayer changes things, and it changes you. Today, instead of turning things over in your mind, turn them over to God in prayer. Instead of worrying about your next decision, ask God to lead the way. Don't limit your prayers to meals or to bedtime; pray constantly. God is listening; He wants to hear from you; and you most certainly need to hear from Him.

Prayer connects us with God's limitless potential.

—

Henry Blackaby

When there is a matter that requires definite prayer, pray until you believe God and until you can thank Him for His answer.

Hannah Whitall Smith

Prayer is not a work that can be allocated to one or another group in the church. It is everybody's responsibility; it is everybody's privilege.

A. W. Tozer

God wants to remind us that nothing on earth or in hell can ultimately stand against the man or the woman who calls on the name of the Lord!

Jim Cymbala

Prayer shouldn't be casual or sporadic, dictated only by the needs of the moment. Prayer should be as much a part of our lives as breathing.

Billy Graham

TODAY'S INTEGRITY BUILDER

Prayer strengthens your character and your relationship with God . . . so pray. Martin Luther observed, "If I should neglect prayer but a single day, I should lose a great deal of the fire of faith." Those words apply to you, too. And it's up to you to live—and to pray—accordingly.

The intense prayer of the righteous is very powerful.

James 5:16 Holman CSB

Let the words of my mouth and the meditation of my heart be acceptable in Your sight, O Lord, my strength and my Redeemer.

Psalm 19:14 NKJV

Yet He often withdrew to deserted places and prayed.

Luke 5:16 Holman CSB

Don't worry about anything, but in everything, through prayer and petition with thanksgiving, let your requests be made known to God.

Philippians 4:6 Holman CSB

TODAY'S PRAYER

Dear Lord, I will open my heart to You. I will take my concerns, my fears, my plans, and my hopes to You in prayer. And, then, I will trust the answers that You give. You are my loving Father, and I will accept Your will for my life today and every day that I live. Amen

DAY 4

FORGIVENESS NOW

*Then Peter came to Him and said, "Lord, how many times
could my brother sin against me and I forgive him?
As many as seven times?" "I tell you, not as many as seven,"
Jesus said to him, "but 70 times seven."*

Matthew 18:21-22 Holman CSB

It has been said that life is an exercise in forgiveness. And it should be added that forgiveness is also an exercise in character building.

Christ understood the importance of forgiveness when he commanded, "Love your enemies and pray for those who persecute you" (Matthew 5:43-44 NIV). But sometimes, forgiveness is difficult indeed.

When we have been injured or embarrassed, we feel the urge to strike back and to hurt the ones who have hurt us. But Christ instructs us to do otherwise. Christ teaches us that forgiveness is God's way and that mercy is an integral part of God's plan for our lives. In short, we are commanded to weave the thread of forgiveness into the very fabric of our lives.

Do you invest more time than you should reliving the past? Are you troubled by feelings of anger, bitterness, envy, or regret? Do you harbor ill will against someone whom you simply can't seem to forgive? If so, it's time to finally get serious about forgiveness.

When someone hurts you, the act of forgiveness is difficult, but necessary. Until you forgive, you are trapped in a prison of your own creation. But what if you have tried to forgive and simply can't seem to do so? The solution to your dilemma is this: you simply must make forgiveness a higher priority in your life.

Most of us don't spend too much time thinking about forgiveness; we worry, instead, about the injustices we have suffered and the people who inflicted them. God has a better plan: He wants us to live in the present, not the past, and He knows that in order to do so, we must forgive those who have harmed us.

Have you made forgiveness a high priority? Have you sincerely asked God to forgive you for your inability to forgive others? Have you genuinely prayed that those feelings of hatred and anger might be swept from your heart? If so, congratulations. If not, perhaps it's time to rearrange your priorities . . . and perhaps it's time to fortify your character by freeing yourself from the chains of bitterness and regret.

As you have received the mercy of God by the forgiveness of sin and the promise of eternal life, thus you must show mercy.

Billy Graham

To be a Christian means to forgive the inexcusable, because God has forgiven the inexcusable in you.

C. S. Lewis

There is always room for more loving forgiveness within our homes.

James Dobson

It is said that forgiveness is the fragrance the violet sheds on the heel that has crushed it. If so, could there be a fragrance as sweet in all the Bible as that of Jesus washing the feet of the very one whose heel was raised against Him?

Charles Swindoll

TODAY'S INTEGRITY BUILDER

Today, make a list of the people you still need to forgive. Then make up your mind to forgive at least one person on that list. Finally, ask God to cleanse your heart of bitterness, animosity, and regret. If you ask Him sincerely and often, He will respond.

Therefore, God's chosen ones, holy and loved, put on heartfelt compassion, kindness, humility, gentleness, and patience, accepting one another and forgiving one another if anyone has a complaint against another. Just as the Lord has forgiven you, so also you must forgive.

Colossians 3:12-13 Holman CSB

And be kind and compassionate to one another, forgiving one another, just as God also forgave you in Christ.

Ephesians 4:32 Holman CSB

And forgive us our sins, for we ourselves also forgive everyone in debt to us. And do not bring us into temptation.

Luke 11:4 NKJV

Be merciful, just as your Father also is merciful.

Luke 6:36 Holman CSB

TODAY'S PRAYER

Heavenly Father, give me a forgiving heart. When I am bitter, Your Word reminds me that forgiveness is Your commandment. Let me be Your obedient servant, Lord, and let me be a man who forgives others just as You have forgiven me. Amen

THE NEED TO LEAD

Good leadership is a channel of water controlled by God;
he directs it to whatever ends he chooses.

Proverbs 21:1 MSG

Harry Truman was the plainspoken American president who said, "If you can't stand the heat, get out of the kitchen." And, he spoke from hard-earned experience. As commander-in-chief during the final days of World War II, the feisty Mr. Truman faced many tough decisions, and he never dodged them. Instead, he followed the advice of another president, Andrew Jackson, who once said, "Take time to deliberate; but when the time for action arrives, stop thinking and go ahead."

Now, if Truman were here, he'd be quick to say that genuine leadership is an exercise in character building, not a popularity contest. Genuine leadership often requires tough decisions, decisions that by their definition, are displeasing to some. But, effective leaders are willing to sacrifice popularity for results.

If you are in a position of leadership—whether at church, home, work, or school—it's up to you to set the right tone by making hard decisions and by setting a proper example. But make no mistake: wise leaders don't make things too serious. The best leaders learn to laugh (when it's appropriate), when to have fun (the good, clean kind), and when to lead (by example, of course).

Are you the kind of leader whom you would want to follow? If so, congratulations. But if the answer to that question is in question, it's time to improve your leadership skills, beginning with the words that you speak and the example that you set.

If you occupy a position of leadership (and you do), then you should prepare yourself for the day (which will probably arrive sooner than you expect) when you will be faced with a tough, unpopular decision. When that day arrives, you have a choice to make: you can either do the right thing or the easy thing. Do the right thing. After all, every kitchen heats up on occasion, so you might as well get used to it. And, the best way to get used to a warm kitchen is to hang in there and take the heat, knowing that every kitchen, in time, cools down. And so will yours.

The test of a leader is taking the vision from me to we.

John Maxwell

What do we Christians chiefly value in our leaders? The answer seems to be not their holiness, but their gifts and skills and resources. The thought that only holy people are likely to be spiritually useful does not loom large in our minds.

J. I. Packer

A wise leader chooses a variety of gifted individuals. He complements his strengths.

Charles Stanley

People who inspire others are those who see invisible bridges at the end of dead-end streets.

Charles Swindoll

TODAY'S INTEGRITY BUILDER

Today, think about your own leadership style. Remember that leadership comes in many forms and that you will probably be more effective using your own style, not by trying to copy someone else. When it comes to leadership, an original version of yourself is far better than a weak imitation of someone else.

According to the grace given to us, we have different gifts: If prophecy, use it according to the standard of faith; if service, in service; if teaching, in teaching; if exhorting, in exhortation; giving, with generosity; leading, with diligence; showing mercy, with cheerfulness.

Romans 12:6-8 Holman CSB

Shepherd God's flock among you, not overseeing out of compulsion but freely, according to God's will; not for the money but eagerly.

1 Peter 5:2 Holman CSB

And we exhort you, brothers: warn those who are lazy, comfort the discouraged, help the weak, be patient with everyone.

1 Thessalonians 5:14 Holman CSB

TODAY'S PRAYER

Dear Lord, when I find myself in a position of leadership, let me seek Your will and obey Your commandments. Make me a man of integrity and wisdom, Lord, and make me a worthy example to those whom I serve. Let me be a Christ-centered leader, and let me turn to You, Father, for guidance, for courage, for wisdom, and for love. Amen

WHAT IS YOUR FOCUS?

*Guard your heart above all else, for it is the source of life.
Don't let your mouth speak dishonestly, and don't let your
lips talk deviously. Let your eyes look forward; fix your gaze
straight ahead. Carefully consider the path for your feet,
and all your ways will be established. Don't turn to the right
or to the left; keep your feet away from evil.*

Proverbs 4:23-27 Holman CSB

The condition of your character is determined, to a surprising extent, by the direction of your thoughts. If you focus your thoughts and energies on matters that honor your God, your family, and yourself, you will reap rich rewards. But if you focus too intently on the distractions and temptations of our 21st-century world, you're inviting large quantities of trouble.

What is your focus today? Are you willing to focus your thoughts and energies on God's blessings and upon His will for your life? Or will you turn your thoughts to other things? Before you answer that question, consider this: God created you in His own image, and He wants you to experience joy and abundance. But, God will not force His joy upon you; you must claim it for yourself.

Today, why not focus your thoughts on the joy that is rightfully yours in Christ? Why not take time to celebrate God's glorious creation? Why not trust your hopes instead of your fears? And why not focus, not on the world's priorities, but on God's priorities. When you do, you'll experience the peace and the power that accrues to those who put Jesus first in their lives.

Is Christ really the focus of your life? Are you fired with enthusiasm for Him? Are you an energized Christian man who allows God's Son to reign over every aspect of your day? Make no mistake: that's exactly what God intends for you to do.

God has given you the gift of eternal life through His Son. In response to God's priceless gift, you are instructed to focus your thoughts, your prayers, and your energies upon God and His only begotten Son. To do so, you must resist the subtle yet powerful temptation to become a "spiritual dabbler."

A person who dabbles in the Christian faith is unwilling to place God in His rightful place: above all other things. Resist that temptation; make God the cornerstone and the touchstone of your life. When you do, He will give you all the strength and wisdom you need to live victoriously for Him.

As long as Jesus is one of many options, he is no option.

Max Lucado

If the glories of heaven were more real to us, if we lived less for material things and more for things eternal and spiritual, we would be less easily disturbed in this present life.

Billy Graham

Give me the person who says, "This one thing I do, and not these fifty things I dabble in."

D. L. Moody

Paul did one thing. Most of us dabble in forty things. Are you a doer or a dabbler?

Vance Havner

TODAY'S INTEGRITY BUILDER

Ask yourself if you're truly focusing your thoughts and energies on matters that are pleasing to God and beneficial to your family. Then ask your Creator to help you focus on His love, His Son, and His plan for your life.

Let us lay aside every weight and the sin that so easily ensnares us, and run with endurance the race that lies before us, keeping our eyes on Jesus, the source and perfecter of our faith.

Hebrews 12:1-2 Holman CSB

Therefore don't worry about tomorrow, because tomorrow will worry about itself. Each day has enough trouble of its own.

Matthew 6:34 Holman CSB

In any case, we should live up to whatever truth we have attained.

Philippians 3:16 Holman CSB

Enter through the narrow gate; because the gate is wide and the road is broad that leads to destruction, and there are many who go through it. How narrow is the gate and difficult the road that leads to life; and few find it.

Matthew 7:13-14 Holman CSB

TODAY'S PRAYER

Dear Lord, help me to face this day with a spirit of optimism and thanksgiving. And let me focus my thoughts on You and Your incomparable gifts. Amen

LIVING ON PURPOSE

*He is the image of the invisible God, the firstborn over
all creation; because by Him everything was created,
in heaven and on earth, the visible and the invisible,
whether thrones or dominions or rulers or authorities—
all things have been created through Him and for Him.*

Colossians 1:15-16 Holman CSB

"What did God put me here to do?" If you're
like most of people, you've asked yourself
that question on many occasions. Perhaps
you have pondered your future, uncertain of your plans,
unsure of your next step. But even if you don't have a clear
plan for the next step of your life's journey, you may rest
assured that God does.

God has a plan for the universe, and He has a plan
for you. He understands that plan as thoroughly and completely as He knows you. If you seek God's will earnestly
and prayerfully, He will make His plans known to you in
His own time and in His own way.

Do you sincerely seek to discover God's purpose for
your life? If so, you must first be willing to live in accordance with His commandments. You must also study

33

God's Word and be watchful for His signs. Finally, you should open yourself up to the Creator every day—beginning with this one—and you must have faith that He will soon reveal His plans to you.

Perhaps your vision of God's purpose for your life has been clouded by a wish list that you have expected God to dutifully fulfill. Perhaps, you have fervently hoped that God would create a world that unfolds according to your wishes, not His. If so, you have experienced more disappointment than satisfaction and more frustration than peace. A better strategy is to conform your will to God's (and not to struggle vainly in an attempt to conform His will to yours).

Sometimes, God's plans and purposes may seem unmistakably clear to you. If so, push ahead. But other times, He may lead you through the wilderness before He directs you to the Promised Land. So be patient and keep seeking His will for your life. When you do, you'll be amazed at the marvelous things that an all-powerful, all-knowing God can do.

When God speaks to you through the Bible, prayer, circumstances, the church, or in some other way, he has a purpose in mind for your life.

Henry Blackaby and Claude King

The greatest tragedy is not death, but life without purpose.

Rick Warren

Let us live with urgency. Let us exploit the opportunity of life. Let us not drift. Let us live intentionally. We must not trifle our lives away.

Raymond Ortlund

Oh Lord, let me not live to be useless.

John Wesley

TODAY'S INTEGRITY BUILDER

Perhaps you're in a hurry to understand God's unfolding plan for your life. If so, remember that God operates according to a perfect timetable. That timetable is His, not yours. So be patient. God has big things in store for you, but He may have quite a few lessons to teach you before you are fully prepared to do His will and fulfill His purpose.

For it is God who is working among you both the willing and the working for His good purpose.

Philippians 2:13 Holman CSB

We know that all things work together for the good of those who love God: those who are called according to His purpose.

Romans 8:28 Holman CSB

I will instruct you and show you the way to go; with My eye on you, I will give counsel.

Psalm 32:8 Holman CSB

You reveal the path of life to me; in Your presence is abundant joy; in Your right hand are eternal pleasures.

Psalm 16:11 Holman CSB

TODAY'S PRAYER

Dear Lord, let Your purposes be my purposes. Let Your priorities be my priorities. Let Your will be my will. Let Your Word be my guide. And, let me grow in faith and in wisdom today and every day. Amen

DAY 8

BEYOND FEAR

*I sought the Lord, and He answered me
and delivered me from all my fears.*

Psalm 34:4 Holman CSB

Norman Vincent Peale had simple advice; he said, "Do not build up obstacles in your imagination. Difficulties must be studied and dealt with, but they must not be magnified by fear." And he was right— the decision to face a fear instead of running from it is always an exercise in character building.

We live in a world that can be, at times, a very frightening place. We live in a world that is, at times, a very discouraging place. We live in a world where life-changing losses can be so painful and so profound that it seems we will never recover. But, with God's help, and with the help of encouraging family members and friends, we can recover.

During the darker days of life, we are wise to remember the words of Jesus, who reassured His disciples, saying, "Take courage! It is I. Don't be afraid" (Matthew 14:27 NIV).

Are you willing to face your fears right now? Are you willing to cast off the chains of timidity and procrastination by deciding to do what needs to be done now, not "later"? If the answer to these questions if yes, then you're destined to build a better life for yourself and your loved ones.

Today, ask God for the courage to step beyond the boundaries of your self-doubts. Ask Him to guide you to a place where you can realize your full potential—a place where you are freed from the fear of failure. Ask Him to do His part, and promise Him that you will do your part. Don't ask Him to lead you to a "safe" place; ask Him to lead you to the "right" place . . . and remember: those two places are seldom the same.

When we meditate on God and remember
the promises He has given us in His Word,
our faith grows, and our fears dissolve.

—

Charles Stanley

The Lord Jesus by His Holy Spirit is with me, and the knowledge of His presence dispels the darkness and allays any fears.

Bill Bright

Fear and doubt are conquered by a faith that rejoices. And faith can rejoice because the promises of God are as certain as God Himself.

Kay Arthur

One of the main missions of God is to free us from the debilitating bonds of fear and anxiety. God's heart is broken when He sees us so demoralized and weighed down by fear.

Bill Hybels

TODAY'S INTEGRITY BUILDER

Are you feeling anxious or fearful? If so, trust God to handle those problems that are simply too big for you to solve. Entrust the future—your future—to God. Then, spend a few minutes thinking about specific steps you can take to confront—and conquer—your fears.

Even when I go through the darkest valley, I fear [no] danger, for You are with me.

Psalm 23:4 Holman CSB

Don't be afraid. Only believe.

Mark 5:36 Holman CSB

For I, the Lord your God, hold your right hand and say to you: Do not fear, I will help you.

Isaiah 41:13 Holman CSB

Do not fear, for I am with you; do not be afraid, for I am your God. I will strengthen you; I will help you; I will hold on to you with My righteous right hand.

Isaiah 41:10 Holman CSB

TODAY'S PRAYER

Your Word reminds me, Lord, that even when I walk through the valley of the shadow of death, I need fear no evil, for You are with me, and You comfort me. Thank You, Lord, for a perfect love that casts out fear. Let me live courageously and faithfully this day and every day. Amen

SHARING YOUR FAITH BUILDS CHARACTER

*But sanctify the Lord God in your hearts,
and always be ready to give a defense to everyone
who asks you a reason for the hope that is in you.*
1 Peter 3:15 Holman CSB

Have you made the decision to allow Christ to reign over your heart? If so, you have an important story to tell: yours.

Your personal testimony is profoundly important, but perhaps because of shyness (or because of the fear of being rebuffed), you've been hesitant to share your experiences. If so, you should start paying less attention to your own insecurities and more attention to the message that God wants you to share with the world.

In his second letter to Timothy, Paul shares a message to believers of every generation when he writes, "God has not given us a spirit of timidity" (1:7 NASB). Paul's meaning is clear: When sharing our testimonies, we must be courageous, forthright, and unashamed.

Corrie ten Boom observed, "There is nothing anybody else can do that can stop God from using us. We can turn everything into a testimony." Her words remind us that when we speak up for God, our actions may speak even more loudly than our words.

When we let other people know the details of our faith, we assume an important responsibility: the responsibility of making certain that our words are reinforced by our actions. When we share our testimonies, we must also be willing to serve as shining examples of righteousness—undeniable examples of the changes that Jesus makes in the lives of those who accept Him as their Savior.

Are you a man who is willing to follow in the footsteps of Jesus? If so, you must also be willing to talk about Him. And make no mistake—the time to express your belief in Him is now. You know how He has touched your own heart; help Him do the same for others.

To stand in an uncaring world and say,
"See, here is the Christ" is a daring act of courage.

—

Calvin Miller

To take up the cross means that you take your stand for the Lord Jesus no matter what it costs.

Billy Graham

Usually it is those who know Him that bring Him to others. That is why the Church, the whole body of Christians showing Him to one another, is so important.

C. S. Lewis

Our Lord is searching for people who will make a difference. Christians dare not dissolve into the background or blend into the neutral scenery of the world.

Charles Swindoll

The sermon of your life in tough times ministers to people more powerfully than the most eloquent speaker.

Bill Bright

TODAY'S INTEGRITY BUILDER

What if you're uncomfortable talking about your faith? Remember: you're not giving the State of the Union Address—you're having a conversation. And besides, if you're not sure what to say, a good place to start is by asking questions, not making speeches.

The following night, the Lord stood by him and said, "Have courage! For as you have testified about Me in Jerusalem, so you must also testify in Rome."

Acts 23:11 Holman CSB

But as for me, I will never boast about anything except the cross of our Lord Jesus Christ, through whom the world has been crucified to me, and I to the world.

Galatians 6:14 Holman CSB

And I say to you, anyone who acknowledges Me before men, the Son of Man will also acknowledge him before the angels of God; but whoever denies Me before men will be denied before the angels of God.

Luke 12:8-9 Holman CSB

Whatever I tell you in the dark, speak in the light; and what you hear in the ear, preach on the housetops.

Matthew 10:27 NKJV

Today's Prayer

Lord, the life that I live and the words that I speak will tell my family and the world how I feel about You. Today and every day, let my testimony be worthy of You. Let my words be sure and true, and let my actions point others to You. Amen

CHARACTER AND MATURITY

*Do not be conformed to this age, but be transformed
by the renewing of your mind, so that you may discern what
is the good, pleasing, and perfect will of God.*

Romans 12:2 Holman CSB

Character-building never happens overnight. To the contrary, the journey toward spiritual maturity lasts a lifetime. As Christians, we can and should continue to grow in the love and the knowledge of our Savior as long as we live. Norman Vincent Peale had the following advice for believers of all ages: "Ask the God who made you to keep remaking you." That advice, of course, is perfectly sound, but often ignored.

When we cease to grow, either emotionally or spiritually, we do ourselves a profound disservice. But, if we study God's Word, if we obey His commandments, and if we live in the center of His will, we will not be "stagnant" believers; we will, instead, be growing Christians . . . and that's exactly what God intends for us to be.

Our lives and our characters are constructed by the countless thoughts and choices we make every day. Each day, we make decisions that can strengthen our characters

. . . or not. When we choose to honor the Creator with our thoughts, our prayers, and our actions, we keep growing day by day . . . and that's precisely what each of us should do.

A Christian is never in a state of completion but always in the process of becoming.

Martin Luther

Integrity and maturity are two character traits vital to the heart of a leader.

Charles Stanley

God's plan for our guidance is for us to grow gradually in wisdom before we get to the cross roads.

Bill Hybels

TODAY'S INTEGRITY BUILDER

Today, think about the quality of the choices that you've made recently. Are these choices helping you become a more mature Christian? If so, don't change. If not, think about the quality of your decisions, the consequences of those decisions, and the steps that you can take to make better decisions.

When I was a child, I spoke like a child, I thought like a child, I reasoned like a child. When I became a man, I put aside childish things.

1 Corinthians 13:11 Holman CSB

Consider it a great joy, my brothers, whenever you experience various trials, knowing that the testing of your faith produces endurance. But endurance must do its complete work, so that you may be mature and complete, lacking nothing.

James 1:2-4 Holman CSB

But grow in the grace and knowledge of our Lord and Savior Jesus Christ. To Him be the glory both now and to the day of eternity.

2 Peter 3:18 Holman CSB

Therefore, leaving the elementary message about the Messiah, let us go on to maturity.

Hebrews 6:1 Holman CSB

TODAY'S PRAYER

Lord, let me grow in Your wisdom. When I study Your Word and follow Your commandments, I become a more mature Christian and a more effective servant for You. Let me grow up, Lord, and let me keep growing up every day that I live. Amen

DAY 11

THE RIGHT KIND OF EXAMPLE?

You should be an example to the believers in speech, in conduct, in love, in faith, in purity.

1 Timothy 4:12 Holman CSB

Whether you know it or not, you're a role model. Your friends and family members watch your actions and make careful mental notes about what those actions reveal about your character. Your obligation, of course, is to behave accordingly. After all, your words of instruction will never ring true unless you yourself are willing to follow them.

What kind of example are you? Are you the kind of person whose life serves as a model of integrity and righteousness? Are you a believer whose behavior serves as a positive role model for others? Are you the kind of Christian whose actions, day in and day out, are based upon kindness, faithfulness, and a love for the Lord? If so, you are not only blessed by God, but you are also a powerful force for good in a world that desperately needs positive influences such as yours.

Corrie ten Boom advised, "Don't worry about what you do not understand. Worry about what you do understand in the Bible but do not live by." And Phillips Brooks advised, "Be such a man, and live such a life, that if every person were such as you, and every life a life like yours, this earth would be God's Paradise." That's sound advice because your family and friends are watching . . . and so, for that matter, is God.

The sermon of your life in tough times
ministers to people more powerfully
than the most eloquent speaker.

—

Bill Bright

We urgently need people who encourage and inspire us to move toward God and away from the world's enticing pleasures.

Jim Cymbala

A holy life will produce the deepest impression. Lighthouses blow no horns; they only shine.

D. L. Moody

Living life with a consistent spiritual walk deeply influences those we love most.

Vonette Bright

Men are mirrors, or "carriers" of Christ to other men. Sometimes unconscious carriers.

C. S. Lewis

TODAY'S INTEGRITY BUILDER

Your life is a sermon. What kind of sermon will you preach? The words you choose to speak may have some impact on others, but not nearly as much impact as the life you choose to live. Today, pause to consider the tone, the theme, and the context of your particular sermon, and ask yourself if it's a message that you're proud to deliver.

Therefore since we also have such a large cloud of witnesses surrounding us, let us lay aside every weight and the sin that so easily ensnares us, and run with endurance the race that lies before us.

Hebrews 12:1 Holman CSB

Set an example of good works yourself, with integrity and dignity in your teaching.

Titus 2:7 Holman CSB

You are the light of the world. A city situated on a hill cannot be hidden. No one lights a lamp and puts it under a basket, but rather on a lampstand, and it gives light for all who are in the house. In the same way, let your light shine before men, so that they may see your good works and give glory to your Father in heaven.

Matthew 5:14-16 Holman CSB

TODAY'S PRAYER

Lord, make me a man who is a worthy example to my family and friends. And, let my words and my deeds serve as a testimony to the changes You have made in my life. Let me praise You, Father, by following in the footsteps of Your Son, and let others see Him through me. Amen

FAITH BUILDS CHARACTER

*I assure you: If anyone says to this mountain,
"Be lifted up and thrown into the sea," and does not
doubt in his heart, but believes that what he says will happen,
it will be done for him.*

Mark 11:23 Holman CSB

Because we live in a demanding world, all of us have mountains to climb and mountains to move. Moving those mountains requires faith. And the experience of trying, with God's help, to move mountains builds character.

Faith, like a tender seedling, can be nurtured or neglected. When we nurture our faith through prayer, meditation, and worship, God blesses our lives and lifts our spirits. But when we neglect to commune with the Father, we do ourselves and our loved ones a profound disservice.

Are you a mountain-moving man whose faith is evident for all to see? Or, are you a spiritual underachiever? As you think about the answer to that question, consider this: God needs more people who are willing to move mountains for His glory and for His kingdom.

Every life—including yours—is a series of wins and losses. Every step of the way, through every triumph and tragedy, God walks with you, ready and willing to strengthen you. So the next time you find your character being tested, remember to take your fears to God. If you call upon Him, you will be comforted. Whatever your challenge, whatever your trouble, God can handle it.

When you place your faith, your trust, indeed your life in the hands of your Heavenly Father, you'll receive a lesson in character-building from the ultimate Teacher. So strengthen your faith through praise, through worship, through Bible study, and through prayer. And trust God's plans. With Him, all things are possible, and He stands ready to open a world of possibilities to you . . . if you have faith.

> Only God can move mountains,
> but faith and prayer can move God.
>
> —
>
> E. M. Bounds

Faith is confidence in the promises of God or confidence that God will do what He has promised.

Charles Stanley

I am truly grateful that faith enables me to move past the question of "Why?"

Zig Ziglar

How do you walk in faith? By claiming the promises of God and obeying the Word of God, in spite of what you see, how you feel, or what may happen.

Warren Wiersbe

It is the trial of our faith that is precious. If we go through the trial, there is so much wealth laid up in our heavenly bank account to draw upon when the next test comes.

Oswald Chambers

TODAY'S INTEGRITY BUILDER

Today, think about the times you've been hesitant to share your faith. And as you contemplate the day ahead, think about three specific ways that you can vocalize your faith to family and friends.

For whatever is born of God overcomes the world. And this is the victory that has overcome the world—our faith.

1 John 5:4 NKJV

Now without faith it is impossible to please God, for the one who draws near to Him must believe that He exists and rewards those who seek Him.

Hebrews 11:6 Holman CSB

Everything is possible to the one who believes.

Mark 9:23 Holman CSB

Pursue righteousness, godliness, faith, love, endurance, and gentleness. Fight the good fight for the faith; take hold of eternal life, to which you were called and have made a good confession before many witnesses.

1 Timothy 6:11-12 Holman CSB

TODAY'S PRAYER

Dear Lord, I want faith that moves mountains. You have big plans for this world and big plans for me. Help me fulfill those plans, Father, as I follow in the footsteps of Your Son. Amen

DAY 13

A WORLD BRIMMING
WITH TEMPTATION

Be sober! Be on the alert!
Your adversary the Devil is prowling around like
a roaring lion, looking for anyone he can devour.

1 Peter 5:8 Holman CSB

I t's inevitable: today you will be tempted by somebody
or something—in fact, you will probably be tempted
on countless occasions. Why? Because you live in a
world that's filled to the brim with temptations and addictions that are intended to lead you far, far away from God.

Here in the 21st century, temptations are now completely and thoroughly woven into the fabric of everyday
life. Seductive images are everywhere; subtle messages tell
you that it's okay to sin "just a little"; and to make matters
even worse, society doesn't just seem to endorse godless-
ness, it actually seems to reward it. Society spews forth a
wide range of messages, all of which imply that it's okay
to rebel against God. These messages, of course, are ex-
tremely dangerous and completely untrue.

How can you stand up against society's tidal wave of
temptations? By learning to direct your thoughts and your

eyes in ways that are pleasing to God . . . and by relying upon Him to deliver you from the evils that threaten you. And here's the good news: the Creator has promised (not implied, not suggested, not insinuated—He has promised!) that with His help, you can resist every single temptation that confronts you.

When it comes to fighting Satan, you are never alone. God is always with you, and if you do your part He will do His part. But what, precisely, is your part? A good starting point is simply learning how to recognize the subtle temptations that surround you. The images of immorality are ubiquitous, and they're intended to hijack your mind, your heart, your pocketbook, your life, and your soul. Don't let them do it.

Satan is both industrious and creative; he's working 24/7, and he's causing pain, heartache, trauma, and tragedy in more ways than ever before. You, as man of God, must remain watchful and strong—starting today, and ending never.

Most Christians do not know or fully realize that the adversary of our lives is Satan and that his main tool is our flesh, our old nature.

Bill Bright

The first step on the way to victory is to recognize the enemy.

Corrie ten Boom

The Devil is a master strategist. He varies his attacks as skillfully as an experienced general and always has one more trick to use against the one who imagines he is well experienced in the holy war.

A. W. Tozer

A man who gives in to temptation after five minutes simply does not know what it would have been like an hour later.

C. S. Lewis

TODAY'S INTEGRITY BUILDER

Ask yourself these important questions: What images, people, or places are you likely to encounter today that might encourage you to think impure thoughts? And how will you prepare yourself to respond to these temptations?

No temptation has overtaken you except what is common to humanity. God is faithful and He will not allow you to be tempted beyond what you are able, but with the temptation He will also provide a way of escape, so that you are able to bear it.

1 Corinthians 10:13 Holman CSB

For we do not have a High Priest who cannot sympathize with our weaknesses, but was in all points tempted as we are, yet without sin. Let us therefore come boldly to the throne of grace, that we may obtain mercy and find grace to help in time of need.

Hebrews 4:15-16 NKJV

Put on the whole armor of God, that you may be able to stand against the wiles of the devil.

Ephesians 6:11 NKJV

Today's Prayer

Lord, life is filled with temptations to stray from Your chosen path. But, I face no temptation that You have not already met and conquered through my Lord and Savior Jesus Christ, the One who empowers me with His strength and His love. Amen

DISCIPLINE BUILDS CHARACTER

But I discipline my body and bring it into subjection,
lest, when I have preached to others,
I myself should become disqualified.
1 Corinthians 9:27 NKJV

God's Word reminds us again and again that our Creator expects us to lead disciplined lives. God doesn't reward laziness, misbehavior, or apathy. To the contrary, He expects us to behave with dignity and discipline. But ours is a world in which dignity and discipline are often in short supply.

We live in a world in which leisure is glorified and indifference is often glamorized. But God has other plans. God gives us talents, and He expects us to use them. But it is not always easy to cultivate those talents. Sometimes, we must invest countless hours (or, in some cases, many years) honing our skills. And that's perfectly okay with God, because He understands that self-discipline is a blessing, not a burden.

Proverbs 23:12 advises: "Apply your heart to discipline And your ears to words of knowledge" (NASB). And, 2

Peter 1:5-6 teaches, "make every effort to supplement your faith with goodness, goodness with knowledge, knowledge with self-control, self-control with endurance, endurance with godliness" (Holman CSB). Thus, God's Word is clear: we must exercise self-discipline in all matters. And as we build self-discipline, we also build character.

When we pause to consider how much work needs to be done, we realize that self-discipline is not simply a proven way to get ahead, it's also an integral part of God's plan for our lives. If we genuinely seek to be faithful stewards of our time, our talents, and our resources, we must adopt a disciplined approach to life. Otherwise, our talents are wasted and our resources are squandered.

Life's greatest rewards seldom fall into our laps; to the contrary, our greatest accomplishments usually require work, perseverance, and discipline. May we, as disciplined believers, be willing to work the rewards we so earnestly desire.

The alternative to discipline is disaster.

—

Vance Havner

If one examines the secret behind a championship football team, a magnificent orchestra, or a successful business, the principal ingredient is invariably discipline.

James Dobson

Personal humility is a spiritual discipline and the hallmark of the service of Jesus.

Franklin Graham

As we seek to become disciples of Jesus Christ, we should never forget that the word *disciple* is directly related to the word *discipline*. To be a disciple of the Lord Jesus Christ is to know his discipline.

Dennis Swanberg

Simply stated, self-discipline is obedience to God's Word and willingness to submit everything in life to His will, for His ultimate glory.

John MacArthur

TODAY'S INTEGRITY BUILDER

A disciplined lifestyle gives you more control: The more disciplined you become, the more you can take control over your life (which, by the way, is far better than letting your life take control over you).

The one who follows instruction is on the path to life, but the one who rejects correction goes astray.

Proverbs 10:17 Holman CSB

If you are wise, you are wise for your own benefit; if you mock, you alone will bear [the consequences]. The woman Folly is rowdy; she is gullible and knows nothing.

Proverbs 9:12-13 Holman CSB

The one who understands a matter finds success, and the one who trusts in the Lord will be happy.

Proverbs 16:20 Holman CSB

My son, do not despise the chastening of the Lord, nor be discouraged when you are rebuked by Him.

Hebrews 12:5 NKJV

TODAY'S PRAYER

Lord, I want to be a disciplined man and a disciplined believer. Let me use my time wisely, and let me teach others by the faithfulness of my conduct, today and every day. Amen

CHOICES THAT BUILD CHARACTER

I have set before you life and death, blessing and curse.
Choose life so that you and your descendants may live, love
the Lord your God, obey Him, and remain faithful to Him.
For He is your life, and He will prolong your life
in the land the Lord swore to give to your fathers
Abraham, Isaac, and Jacob.

Deuteronomy 30:19-20 Holman CSB

Life is a series of choices. From the instant we wake in the morning until the moment we nod off to sleep at night, we make countless decisions: decisions about the things we do, decisions about the words we speak, and decisions about the thoughts we choose to think. Simply put, the quality of those decisions determines quality of our lives.

As believers who have been saved by a loving and merciful God, we have every reason to make wise choices. Yet sometimes, amid the inevitable hustle and bustle of life here on earth, we allow ourselves to behave in ways that we know are displeasing to our Creator. When we do, we forfeit the joy and the peace that we might otherwise experience through Him.

As you consider the next step in your life's journey, take time to consider how many things in this life you can control: your thoughts, your words, your priorities, and your actions, for starters. And then, if you sincerely want to discover God's purpose for your life, make choices that are pleasing to Him. He deserves no less . . . and neither do you.

Sometimes, because you're an imperfect human being, you may become so wrapped up in meeting society's expectations that you fail to focus on God's expectations. To do so is a mistake of major proportions—don't make it. Instead, seek God's guidance as you focus your energies on becoming the best "you" that you can possibly be. And, when it comes to matters of conscience, seek approval not from your peers, but from your Creator.

Whom will you try to please today: God or man? Your primary obligation is not to please imperfect men and women. Your obligation is to strive diligently to meet the expectations of an all-knowing and perfect God. Trust Him always. Love Him always. Praise Him always. And make choices that please Him. Always.

Life is pretty much like a cafeteria line—it offers us many choices, both good and bad. The Christian must have a spiritual radar that detects the difference not only between bad and good but also among good, better, and best.

Dennis Swanberg

TODAY'S INTEGRITY BUILDER

First you'll make choices . . . and before you know it, your choices will make you. So take time to think carefully about the direction of your life and the choices that you've been making. Then, try to come up with at least one "new and improved" choice that you can make today.

But seek first the kingdom of God and His righteousness, and all these things shall be added to you.

Matthew 6:33 NKJV

TODAY'S PRAYER

Heavenly Father, I have many choices to make. Help me choose wisely as I follow in the footsteps of Your only begotten Son. Amen

STUDYING GOD'S WORD BUILDS CHARACTER

You will be a good servant of Christ Jesus,
nourished by the words of the faith and of the good teaching
that you have followed.

1 Timothy 4:6 Holman CSB

God's promises are found in a book like no other: the Holy Bible. The Bible is a roadmap for life here on earth and for life eternal. As Christians, we are called upon to trust its promises, to follow its commandments, and to share its Good News.

As believers, we must study the Bible each day and meditate upon its meaning for our lives. Otherwise, we deprive ourselves of an invaluable, character-building gift from the Creator. God's Holy Word is, indeed, a transforming, life-changing, one-of-a-kind treasure. And, a passing acquaintance with the Good Book is insufficient for Christians who seek to obey God's Word and to understand His will.

God has made promises to mankind and to you. God's promises never fail and they never grow old. You must trust those promises and share them with your family, with your friends, and with the world.

Are you standing on the promises of God? Are you expecting God to do wonderful things, or are you living beneath a cloud of apprehension and doubt? The familiar words of Psalm 118:24 remind us of a profound yet simple truth: "This is the day which the LORD hath made; we will rejoice and be glad in it" (KJV). Do you trust that promise, and do you live accordingly? If so, you are living the passionate life that God intends.

For passionate believers, every day begins and ends with God's Son and God's promises. When we accept Christ into our hearts, God promises us the opportunity for earthly peace and spiritual abundance. But more importantly, God promises us the priceless gift of eternal life.

As we face the inevitable challenges of life-here-on-earth, we must arm ourselves with the promises of God's Holy Word. When we do, we can expect the best, not only for the day ahead, but also for all eternity.

Reading news without reading the Bible will inevitably lead to an unbalanced life, an anxious spirit, a worried and depressed soul.

Bill Bright

God gives us a compass and a Book of promises and principles—the Bible—and lets us make our decisions day by day as we sense the leading of His Spirit. This is how we grow.

Warren Wiersbe

The Bible is God's Word, given to us by God Himself so we can know Him and His will for our lives.

Billy Graham

You should not believe your conscience and your feelings more than the word which the Lord who receives sinners preaches to you.

Martin Luther

TODAY'S INTEGRITY BUILDER

Trust God's Word: Charles Swindoll writes, "There are four words I wish we would never forget, and they are, 'God keeps his word.'" And remember: When it comes to studying God's Word, school is always in session.

Heaven and earth will pass away, but My words will never pass away.

Matthew 24:35 Holman CSB

But the word of the Lord endures forever. And this is the word that was preached as the gospel to you.

1 Peter 1:25 Holman CSB

All Scripture is inspired by God and is profitable for teaching, for rebuking, for correcting, for training in righteousness, so that the man of God may be complete, equipped for every good work.

2 Timothy 3:16-17 Holman CSB

For the word of God is living and effective and sharper than any two-edged sword, penetrating as far as to divide soul, spirit, joints, and marrow; it is a judge of the ideas and thoughts of the heart.

Hebrews 4:12 Holman CSB

TODAY'S PRAYER

Heavenly Father, Your Word is a light unto the world; I will study it and trust it, and share it. In all that I do, help me be a worthy witness for You as I share the Good News of Your perfect Son and Your perfect Word. Amen

DAY 17

OPTIMISM BUILDS CHARACTER

I am able to do all things through Him who strengthens me.
Philippians 4:13 Holman CSB

As each day unfolds, you are quite literally surrounded by more opportunities than you can count—opportunities to improve your own life and the lives of those you love. God's Word promises that you, like all of His children, possess the ability to experience earthly peace and spiritual abundance. Yet sometimes—especially if you dwell upon the inevitable disappointments that may, at times, befall even the luckiest among us—you may allow pessimism to invade your thoughts and your heart.

The 19th-century American poet Ella Wheeler Wilcox wrote a poem entitled "Optimism" in which she advised, "Say that you are well and all is well with you, and God will hear your words and make them true." Wilcox understood that optimism is, most often, a matter of intention. If you make the decision to think optimistically, if you purposefully direct your thoughts in positive directions, then you'll enhance your chances of achieving success.

It's undeniable: the self-fulfilling prophecy is alive, well, and living at your house. If you constantly anticipate the worst, that's what you're likely to attract. But, if you make the effort to think positive thoughts, you'll increase the probability that those positive thoughts will come true.

So here's a simple, character-building tip for improving your life: put the self-fulfilling prophecy to work for you. Expect the best, and then get busy working to achieve it. When you do, you'll not only increase the odds of achieving your dreams, but you'll also have more fun along the way.

Christ can put a spring in your step and
a thrill in your heart. Optimism and cheerfulness
are products of knowing Christ.

—

Billy Graham

The popular idea of faith is of a certain obstinate optimism: the hope, tenaciously held in the face of trouble, that the universe is fundamentally friendly and things may get better.

J. I. Packer

It is a remarkable thing that some of the most optimistic and enthusiastic people you will meet are those who have been through intense suffering.

Warren Wiersbe

The essence of optimism is that it takes no account of the present, but it is a source of inspiration, of vitality, and of hope. Where others have resigned, it enables a man to hold his head high, to claim the future for himself, and not abandon it to his enemy.

Dietrich Bonhoeffer

TODAY'S INTEGRITY BUILDER

Be a realistic optimist. Your attitude toward the future will help create your future. So think realistically about yourself and your situation while making a conscious effort to focus on hopes, not fears. When you do, you'll put the self-fulfilling prophecy to work for you.

Make me hear joy and gladness.

Psalm 51:8 NKJV

My cup runs over. Surely goodness and mercy shall follow me all the days of my life; and I will dwell in the house of the Lord Forever.

Psalm 23:5-6 NKJV

But if we hope for what we do not see, we eagerly wait for it with patience.

Romans 8:25 Holman CSB

For God has not given us a spirit of fearfulness, but one of power, love, and sound judgment.

2 Timothy 1:7 Holman CSB

TODAY'S PRAYER

Lord, You care for me, You love me, and You have given me the priceless gift of eternal life through Your Son Jesus. Because of You, Lord, I have every reason to live each day with celebration and hope. Help me to face this day with a spirit of optimism and thanksgiving so that I may lift the spirits of those I meet as I share the Good News of Your Son. And, let me focus my thoughts on You and Your incomparable gifts today and forever. Amen

DAY 18

ADVERSITY BUILDS CHARACTER

God is our refuge and strength, a very present help in trouble.
Psalm 46:1 NKJV

As life here on earth unfolds, all of us encounter occasional disappointments and setbacks: Those occasional visits from Old Man Trouble are simply a fact of life, and none of us are exempt. When tough times arrive, we may be forced to rearrange our plans and our priorities. But even on our darkest days, we must remember that God's love remains constant. And we must never forget that God intends for us to use our setbacks as stepping stones on the path to a better life.

The fact that we encounter adversity is not nearly so important as the way we choose to deal with it. When tough times arrive, we have a clear choice: we can begin the difficult work of tackling our troubles . . . or not. When we summon the courage to look Old Man Trouble squarely in the eye, he usually blinks. But, if we refuse to address our problems, even the smallest annoyances have a way of growing into king-sized catastrophes.

Psalm 145 promises, "The Lord is near to all who call on him, to all who call on him in truth. He fulfills the desires of those who fear him; he hears their cry and saves them" (vv. 18-20 NIV). And the words of Jesus offer us comfort: "These things I have spoken to you, that in Me you may have peace. In the world you will have tribulation; but be of good cheer, I have overcome the world" (John 16:33 NKJV).

As believers, we know that God loves us and that He will protect us. In times of hardship, He will comfort us; in times of sorrow, He will dry our tears. When we are troubled, or weak, or sorrowful, God is always with us. We must build our lives on the rock that cannot be shaken: we must trust in God. And then, we must get on with the character-building, life-altering work of tackling our problems . . . because if we don't, who will? Or should?

Your greatest ministry will likely
come out of your greatest hurt.

—

Rick Warren

God will not permit any troubles to come upon us unless He has a specific plan by which great blessing can come out of the difficulty.

Peter Marshall

Jesus does not say, "There is no storm." He says, I am here, do not toss, but trust."

Vance Havner

As we wait on God, He helps us use the winds of adversity to soar above our problems. As the Bible says, "Those who wait on the LORD . . . shall mount up with wings like eagles."

Billy Graham

TODAY'S INTEGRITY BUILDER

If you're having tough times, don't hit the panic button and don't keep everything bottled up inside. Talk things over with people you can really trust. A second opinion (or, for that matter, a third, fourth, or fifth opinion) is usually helpful. So if your troubles seem overwhelming, be willing to seek outside help—starting, of course, with your pastor.

We also rejoice in our afflictions, because we know that affliction produces endurance, endurance produces proven character, and proven character produces hope.

Romans 5:3-4 Holman CSB

The Lord is a refuge for the oppressed, a refuge in times of trouble.

Psalm 9:9 Holman CSB

For You delivered me from death, even my feet from stumbling, to walk before God in the light of life.

Psalm 56:13 Holman CSB

Be anxious for nothing, but in everything by prayer and supplication, with thanksgiving, let your requests be made known to God.

Philippians 4:6 NKJV

TODAY'S PRAYER

Heavenly Father, You are my strength and my refuge. As I journey through this day, I know that I may encounter disappointments and losses. When I am troubled, let me turn to You. Keep me steady, Lord, and renew a right spirit inside of me this day and forever. Amen

DAY 19

FRIENDS WHO HONOR GOD

Greater love has no one than this,
that he lay down his life for his friends.
John 15:13 NIV

The dictionary defines the word "friend" as "a person who is attached to another by feelings of affection or personal regard." This definition is accurate, as far as it goes, but when we examine the deeper meaning of friendship, many more descriptors come to mind: trustworthiness, loyalty, helpfulness, kindness, understanding, forgiveness, encouragement, humor, and cheerfulness, to mention but a few. Needless to say, our trusted friends and family members can help us discover God's unfolding purposes for our lives. Our task is to enlist our friends' wisdom, their cooperation, their honesty, and their encouragement.

If you genuinely want to strengthen your character, you need to build closer relationships with people who want to do the same. That's why fellowship with likeminded believers should be an integral part of your life. Your friendships should be uplifting, enlightening, encouraging, and (above all) character-building.

Are your friends the kind of men who encourage you to seek God's will and to obey God's Word? If so, you're choosing your friends wisely.

When you build lasting friendships that are pleasing to God, friendships with godly men and women whose values are admirable and whose intentions are honorable, you will be richly blessed. But if you find yourself spending time with folks whose priorities are as questionable as their ethics, you're treading on dangerous ground. So here's an invaluable tip for character building: be careful, very careful, how you choose your friends.

As you're making friendships, be less concerned with appearances and more concerned with integrity. Resolve to be a trustworthy, encouraging, loyal friend to others. And make sure that you appreciate the genuine friends who, by their presence and their love, make you a better person. Friendship is, after all, a glorious gift, praised by God. Give thanks for that gift and nurture it.

God often keeps us on the path by guiding us through the counsel of friends and trusted spiritual advisors.

Bill Hybels

True friends don't spend time gazing into each other's eyes. They show great tenderness toward each other, but they face in the same direction, toward common projects, interest, goals, and above all, toward a common Lord.

C. S. Lewis

Do you want to be wise? Choose wise friends.

Charles Swindoll

A friend who loves will be more concerned about what is best for you than being accepted by you.

Charles Stanley

Today's Integrity Builder

Today, as you think about the nature and the quality of your friendships, remember the first rule of making (and keeping) friends: it's the Golden Rule, and it starts like this: "Do unto others . . . ."

I give thanks to my God for every remembrance of you.

Philippians 1:3 Holman CSB

Beloved, if God so loved us, we also ought to love one another.

1 John 4:11 NKJV

A friend loves at all times, and a brother is born for a difficult time.

Proverbs 17:17 Holman CSB

Iron sharpens iron, and one man sharpens another.

Proverbs 27:17 Holman CSB

TODAY'S PRAYER

Dear Lord, I thank You for my friends. You have brought wonderful Christian friends into my life. Let our friendships honor You as we walk in the footsteps of Your Son. Amen

ENTHUSIASM, PROPERLY DIRECTED, BUILDS CHARACTER

Whatever you do, do it enthusiastically,
as something done for the Lord and not for men.

Colossians 3:23 Holman CSB

Are you passionate about your faith, your life, your family, and your future? Hopefully so. But if your zest for life has waned, it is now time to redirect your efforts and recharge your spiritual batteries. And that means refocusing your priorities by putting God first.

Each day is a glorious opportunity to serve God and to do His will. Are you enthused about life, or do you struggle through each day giving scarcely a thought to God's blessings? Are you constantly praising God for His gifts, and are you sharing His Good News with the world? And are you excited about the possibilities for service that God has placed before you, whether at home, at work, or at church? You should be.

Nothing is more important than your wholehearted commitment to your Creator and to His only begotten

Son. Your faith must never be an afterthought; it must be your ultimate priority, your ultimate possession, and your ultimate passion. When you become passionate about your faith, you'll become passionate about your life, too.

Norman Vincent Peale advised, "Get absolutely enthralled with something. Throw yourself into it with abandon. Get out of yourself. Be somebody. Do something." His words apply to you. So don't settle for a lukewarm existence. Instead, make the character-building choice to become genuinely involved in life. The world needs your enthusiasm . . . and so do you.

Catch on fire with enthusiasm and
people will come for miles to watch you burn.

—

John Wesley

When we wholeheartedly commit ourselves to God, there is nothing mediocre or run-of-the-mill about us. To live for Christ is to be passionate about our Lord and about our lives.

Jim Gallery

Wherever you are, be all there. Live to the hilt every situation you believe to be the will of God.

Jim Elliot

It is a remarkable thing that some of the most optimistic and enthusiastic people you will meet are those who have been through intense suffering.

Warren Wiersbe

Your enthusiasm will be infectious, stimulating, and attractive to others. They will love you for it. They will go for you and with you.

Norman Vincent Peale

TODAY'S INTEGRITY BUILDER

Don't wait for enthusiasm to find you . . . go looking for it. Look at your life and your relationships as exciting adventures. Don't wait for life to spice itself; spice things up yourself.

Do not lack diligence; be fervent in spirit; serve the Lord.

Romans 12:11 Holman CSB

Whatever your hands find to do, do with [all] your strength.

Ecclesiastes 9:10 Holman CSB

I have seen that there is nothing better than for a person to enjoy his activities, because that is his reward. For who can enable him to see what will happen after he dies?

Ecclesiastes 3:22 Holman CSB

Don't work only while being watched, in order to please men, but as slaves of Christ, do God's will from your heart. Render service with a good attitude, as to the Lord and not to men.

Ephesians 6:6-7 Holman CSB

TODAY'S PRAYER

Dear Lord, You have called me not to a life of mediocrity, but to a life of passion. Today, I will be an enthusiastic follower of Your Son, and I will share His Good News—and His love—with all who cross my path. Amen

DO IT NOW;
BUILD CHARACTER NOW

When you make a vow to God, don't delay fulfilling it,
because He does not delight in fools. Fulfill what you vow.
Ecclesiastes 5:4 Holman CSB

The old saying is both familiar and true: actions speak louder than words. And as believers, we must beware: our actions should always give credence to the changes that Christ can make in the lives of those who walk with Him.

God calls upon each of us to act in accordance with His will and with respect for His commandments. If we are to be responsible believers, we must realize that it is never enough to hear the instructions of God; we must also live by them. And it is never enough to wait idly by while others do God's work here on earth; we, too, must act. Doing God's work is a responsibility that each of us must bear, and when we do, we build character moment by moment, day by day.

Are you in the habit of doing what needs to be done when it needs to be done, or are you a dues-paying member of the Procrastinator's Club? If you've acquired the habit of doing things sooner rather than later, congratulations! But, if you find yourself putting off all those unpleasant tasks until later (or never), it's time to think about the consequences of your behavior.

One way that you can learn to defeat procrastination is by paying less attention to your fears and more attention to your responsibilities. So, when you're faced with a difficult choice or an unpleasant responsibility, don't spend endless hours fretting over your fate. Simply seek God's counsel and get busy. When you do, you will be richly rewarded because of your willingness to act.

Do noble things, do not dream them all day long.

—

Charles Kingsley

Every time you refuse to face up to life and its problems, you weaken your character.

E. Stanley Jones

Action springs not from thought, but from a readiness for responsibility.

Dietrich Bonhoeffer

If doing a good act in public will excite others to do more good, then "Let your Light shine to all." Miss no opportunity to do good.

John Wesley

Now is the only time worth having because, indeed, it is the only time we have.

C. H. Spurgeon

Today's Integrity Builder

Today, pick out one important obligation that you've been putting off. Then, take at least one specific step toward the completion of the task you've been avoiding. Even if you don't finish the job, you'll discover that it's easier to finish a job that you've already begun than to finish a job that you've never started.

For the kingdom of God is not in talk but in power.

1 Corinthians 4:20 Holman CSB

Therefore, get your minds ready for action, being self-disciplined, and set your hope completely on the grace to be brought to you at the revelation of Jesus Christ.

1 Peter 1:13 Holman CSB

But be doers of the word and not hearers only.

James 1:22 Holman CSB

Who is wise and understanding among you? He should show his works by good conduct with wisdom's gentleness.

James 3:13 Holman CSB

TODAY'S PRAYER

Dear Lord, today is a new day. Help me tackle the important tasks immediately, even if those tasks are unpleasant. Don't let me put off until tomorrow what I should do today. Amen

DAY 22

CONTROLLING THE DIRECTION OF YOUR THOUGHTS

Therefore, get your minds ready for action, being self-disciplined, and set your hope completely on the grace to be brought to you at the revelation of Jesus Christ.

1 Peter 1:13 Holman CSB

Here's a proven way to build character: learn to control the direction of your thoughts. Your thoughts, of course, are intensely powerful things. Your thoughts have the power to lift you up or drag you down; they have the power to energize you or deplete you, to inspire you to greater accomplishments or to make those accomplishments impossible.

How will you and your family members direct your thoughts today? Will you obey the words of Philippians 4:8 by dwelling upon those things that are honorable, true, and worthy of praise? Or will you allow your thoughts to be hijacked by the negativity that seems to dominate our troubled world?

Are you fearful, angry, bored, or worried? Are you one of those men who is so preoccupied with the concerns of this day that you fail to thank God for the promise of eternity? Are you confused, bitter, or pessimistic? If so, God wants to have a little talk with you.

It's up to you and your loved ones to celebrate the life that God has given you by focusing your minds upon "whatever is commendable." So form the habit of spending more time thinking about your blessings and less time fretting about your hardships. Then, take time to thank the Giver of all things good for gifts that are, in truth, far too numerous to count.

God's cure for evil thinking is to fill our minds
with that which is good.

—

George Sweeting

The mind is like a clock that is constantly running down. It has to be wound up daily with good thoughts.

Fulton J. Sheen

Your thoughts are the determining factor as to whose mold you are conformed to. Control your thoughts and you control the direction of your life.

Charles Stanley

If our minds are stayed upon God, His peace will rule the affairs entertained by our minds. If, on the other hand, we allow our minds to dwell on the cares of this world, God's peace will be far from our thoughts.

Woodroll Kroll

It is the thoughts and intents of the heart that shape a person's life.

John Eldredge

TODAY'S INTEGRITY BUILDER

Watch what you think. If your inner voice is, in reality, your inner critic, you need to tone down the criticism now. And while you're at it, train yourself to begin thinking thoughts that are more rational, more accepting, and less judgmental.

Draw near to God, and He will draw near to you.

James 4:8 Holman CSB

Blessed are the pure in heart, because they will see God.

Matthew 5:8 Holman CSB

Finally brothers, whatever is true, whatever is honorable, whatever is just, whatever is pure, whatever is lovely, whatever is commendable—if there is any moral excellence and if there is any praise—dwell on these things.

Philippians 4:8 Holman CSB

Dear friend, guard Clear Thinking and Common Sense with your life; don't for a minute lose sight of them. They'll keep your soul alive and well, they'll keep you fit and attractive.

Proverbs 3:21-22 MSG

TODAY'S PRAYER

Dear Lord, I will focus on Your love, Your power, Your promises, and Your Son. When I am weak, I will turn to You for strength; when I am worried, I will turn to You for comfort; when I am troubled, I will turn to You for patience and perspective. Help me guard my thoughts, Lord, so that I may honor You this day and forever. Amen

A WILLINGNESS TO SERVE

For I have given you an example that you
also should do just as I have done for you.

John 13:15 Holman CSB

We live in a world that glorifies power, prestige, fame, and money. But the words of Jesus teach us that the most esteemed men are not the widely acclaimed leaders of society; the most esteemed among us are the humble servants of society.

Dietrich Bonhoeffer was correct when he observed, "It is very easy to overestimate the importance of our own achievements in comparison with what we owe others." In other words, reality breeds humility . . . and humility should breed service.

Every single day of your life, including this one, God will give you opportunities to serve Him by serving other people. Welcome those opportunities with open arms. Always be willing to pitch in and make the world a better place, and forego the temptation to keep all your blessings to yourself. When you do, you'll earn rewards that are simply unavailable to folks who stubbornly refuse to serve.

Service is a character-building experience: the more you serve, the more you grow. So, as you go about your daily activities, remember this: the Savior of all humanity made Himself a servant . . . and if you want to really know Him better, you must do the same.

If doing a good act in public will excite others
to do more good, then "Let your Light shine to all."
Miss no opportunity to do good.

—

John Wesley

In Jesus, the service of God and the service of the least of the brethren were one.

Dietrich Bonhoeffer

God wants us to serve Him with a willing spirit, one that would choose no other way.

Beth Moore

If you aren't serving, you're just existing, because life is meant for ministry.

Rick Warren

Make it a rule, and pray to God to help you to keep it, never, if possible, to lie down at night without being able to say: "I have made one human being at least a little wiser, or a little happier, or at least a little better this day."

Charles Kingsley

TODAY'S INTEGRITY BUILDER

Whatever your age, whatever your circumstances, you can serve: Each stage of life's journey is a glorious opportunity to place yourself in the service of the One who is the Giver of all blessings. As long as you live, you should honor God with your service to others.

Therefore, get your minds ready for action, being self-disciplined, and set your hope completely on the grace to be brought to you at the revelation of Jesus Christ.

1 Peter 1:13 Holman CSB

Now there are different gifts, but the same Spirit. There are different ministries, but the same Lord.

1 Corinthians 12:4-5 Holman CSB

Therefore, since we are receiving a kingdom that cannot be shaken, let us hold on to grace. By it, we may serve God acceptably, with reverence and awe.

Hebrews 12:28 Holman CSB

If they serve Him obediently, they will end their days in prosperity and their years in happiness.

Job 36:11 Holman CSB

TODAY'S PRAYER

Dear Lord, when Jesus humbled Himself and became a servant, He also became an example for me. Make me a faithful steward of my gifts, and let me be a humble servant to my loved ones, to my friends, and to those in need. Amen

OBEDIENCE BUILDS CHARACTER

Not everyone who says to Me, "Lord, Lord!"
will enter the kingdom of heaven, but the one who does
the will of My Father in heaven.
Matthew 7:21 Holman CSB

Obedience to God is determined not by words, but by deeds. Talking about righteousness is easy; living righteously is far more difficult, especially in today's temptation-filled world.

Since God created Adam and Eve, we human beings have been rebelling against our Creator. Why? Because we are unwilling to trust God's Word, and we are unwilling to follow His commandments. God has given us a guidebook for righteous living called the Holy Bible. It contains thorough instructions which, if followed, lead to fulfillment, abundance, and salvation. But, if we choose to ignore God's commandments, the results are as predictable as they are tragic.

When we obey God—and when we spend time with friends who do the same—we enjoy profound spiritual rewards. When we behave ourselves as godly men, we strengthen our character by honoring the Creator. When we live righteously and according to God's commandments, He blesses us in ways that we cannot fully understand.

Do you seek God's peace and His blessings? Then obey Him. When you're faced with a difficult choice or a powerful temptation, seek God's counsel and trust the counsel He gives. Invite God into your heart and live according to His commandments. When you do, you will be blessed today, and tomorrow, and forever.

Obedience is the outward expression
of your love of God.

—

Henry Blackaby

Believe and do what God says. The life-changing consequences will be limitless, and the results will be confidence and peace of mind.

Franklin Graham

All true knowledge of God is born out of obedience.

John Calvin

Obedience is the outward expression of your love of God.

Henry Blackaby

Let me tell you—there is no "high" like the elation and joy that come from a sacrificial act of obedience.

Bill Hybels

Obedience that is not motivated by love cannot produce the spiritual fruit that God wants from His children.

Warren Wiersbe

TODAY'S INTEGRITY BUILDER

Obedience leads to spiritual growth. Oswald Chambers correctly observed, "We grow spiritually as our Lord grew physically: by a life of simple, unobtrusive obedience." When you take these words to heart, you will embark upon a lifetime of spiritual growth . . . and God will smile.

You must follow the Lord your God and fear Him. You must keep His commands and listen to His voice; you must worship Him and remain faithful to Him.

Deuteronomy 13:4 Holman CSB

And the world with its lust is passing away, but the one who does God's will remains forever.

1 John 2:17 Holman CSB

Therefore, get your minds ready for action, being self-disciplined, and set your hope completely on the grace to be brought to you at the revelation of Jesus Christ. As obedient children, do not be conformed to the desires of your former ignorance but, as the One who called you is holy, you also are to be holy in all your conduct.

1 Peter 1:13-15 Holman CSB

TODAY'S PRAYER

Lord, my family is both a priceless gift and a profound responsibility. Let my actions be worthy of that responsibility. Lead me along Your path, Lord, and guide me far from the frustrations and distractions of this troubled world. Let Your Holy Word guide my actions, and let Your love reside in my heart, this day and every day. Amen

THE MEDIA TEARS DOWN CHARACTER

Set your minds on what is above, not on what is on the earth.

Colossians 3:2 Holman CSB

Sometimes it's hard to hold on to your integrity, especially when the world keeps pumping out messages that are contrary to your faith and destructive to your character.

The media is working around the clock in an attempt to rearrange your priorities. The media says that possessions are all-important and that "fun" is the ultimate object of life. But guess what? Those messages are lies. The important things in your life have little to do with parties or appearances. The all-important things in life have to do with your faith, your family, and your future. Period.

Are you willing to make the character-building decision to stand up for your faith? If so, you'll be doing yourself a monumental favor. And consider this: When you begin to speak up for God, isn't it logical to assume that you'll also begin to know Him in a more meaningful way? Of course you will.

So forget the media hype, and pay attention to God. Stand up for Him and be counted, not just in church where it's relatively easy to be a Christian, but also outside the church, where it's significantly harder. You owe it God . . . and just as importantly, you owe it to yourself.

The more we stuff ourselves with material pleasures, the less we seem to appreciate life.

Barbara Johnson

It is impossible to please God doing things motivated by and produced by the flesh.

Bill Bright

TODAY'S INTEGRITY BUILDER

Don't Trust the Media's Messages: Many of the messages that you receive from the media are specifically designed to sell you products that interfere with your spiritual, physical, or emotional health. God takes great interest in your health; the moguls from Madison Avenue take great interest in your pocketbook. Trust God.

Let no one deceive himself. If anyone among you seems to be wise in this age, let him become a fool that he may become wise. For the wisdom of this world is foolishness with God. For it is written, "He catches the wise in their own craftiness."

1 Corinthians 3:18–19 NKJV

Do not love the world or the things that belong to the world. If anyone loves the world, love for the Father is not in him.

1 John 2:15 Holman CSB

For whatever is born of God overcomes the world. And this is the victory that has overcome the world—our faith.

1 John 5:4 NKJV

Pure and undefiled religion before our God and Father is this: to look after orphans and widows in their distress and to keep oneself unstained by the world.

James 1:27 Holman CSB

TODAY'S PRAYER

Lord, this world is a dangerous place, and I have many opportunities to stray from your commandments. Help me turn to obey you! Let me keep Christ in my heart, and let me put the devil in his place: far away from me! Amen

DEMONSTRATING YOUR THEOLOGY

Lead a tranquil and quiet life in all godliness and dignity.
1 Timothy 2:2 Holman CSB

Oswald Chambers, the author of the Christian classic *My Utmost for His Highest,* advised, "Never support an experience which does not have God as its source, and faith in God as its result." These words serve as a powerful reminder that, as Christians, we are called to walk with God and obey His commandments. But, we live in a world that presents countless temptations for adults and young people alike.

We Christians, when confronted with sin, have clear instructions: walk—or better yet run—in the opposite direction. When we do, we reap the blessings that God has promised to all those who live according to His will and His word.

As thoughtful adults, we should strive to ensure that our actions are accurate reflections of our beliefs. Our theology must be demonstrated not only by our words but, more importantly, by our actions. In short, we should be practical, conscientious, and quick to act whenever we see an opportunity to serve God.

Today, it's worth considering that your life—how you behave yourself in those day-to-day interactions with family, friends, acquaintances, and even strangers—is an accurate reflection of your creed. If this fact gives you cause for concern, don't bother talking about the changes that you intend to make—make them. And then, when your good deeds speak for themselves—as they most certainly will—don't interrupt.

Either God's Word keeps you from sin,
or sin keeps you from God's Word.

—

Corrie ten Boom

Although our actions have nothing to do with gaining our own salvation, they might be used by God to save somebody else! What we do really matters, and it can affect the eternities of people we care about.

Bill Hybels

Live in such a way that any day would make a suitable capstone for life. Live so that you need not change your mode of living, even if your sudden departure were immediately predicted to you.

C. H. Spurgeon

If we have the true love of God in our hearts, we will show it in our lives. We will not have to go up and down the earth proclaiming it. We will show it in everything we say or do.

D. L. Moody

TODAY'S INTEGRITY BUILDER

Ask yourself if your behavior has been radically changed by your unfolding relationship with God. If the answer to this question is unclear to you—or if the honest answer is a resounding no—think of a single step you can take, a positive change in your life, that will bring you closer to your Creator.

As obedient children, do not be conformed to the desires of your former ignorance but, as the One who called you is holy, you also are to be holy in all your conduct.

1 Peter 1:14-15 Holman CSB

For this very reason, make every effort to supplement your faith with goodness, goodness with knowledge, knowledge with self-control, self-control with endurance, endurance with godliness.

2 Peter 1:5-6 Holman CSB

Therefore as you have received Christ Jesus the Lord, walk in Him.

Colossians 2:6 Holman CSB

Who is wise and understanding among you? He should show his works by good conduct with wisdom's gentleness.

James 3:13 Holman CSB

TODAY'S PRAYER

Lord, there is a right way and a wrong way to live. Let me live according to Your rules, not the world's rules. Your path is right for me, God; let me follow it every day of my life. Amen

STAYING OFF
THE SLIPPERY SLOPE

Jesus responded, "I assure you:
Everyone who commits sin is a slave of sin."
John 8:34 Holman CSB

The temptations of the world sit atop a slippery slope. If you sample those temptations even once, you're on that slope. Perhaps, if you're lucky, you can keep your footing. Perhaps not. But of this you can be certain: if you never step foot on the slippery slope of sin, you'll never slide off.

You live in a world that encourages you to "try" any number of things which are dangerous to your spiritual, mental, or physical health. It's a world brimming with traps and temptations designed to corrupt your character, ruin your health, sabotage your relationships, and wreck your life. And by the way, you know precisely which temptations are most tempting to you, and are therefore the most dangerous.

Invariably, addictive substances and destructive behaviors are described, at least in the beginning, as "harmless" pleasures, but they're not. So your job, as a rational person and a well-meaning Christian, is to do the following: Never experiment with an activity that you wouldn't want to become a full-blown habit. Why? Because when it comes to the temptations of this world, it's easier to stay out than to get out. In other words, the best time to cure a bad habit is before it starts.

There is nothing wrong with asking God's direction.
But it is wrong to go our own way,
then expect Him to bail us out.

—

Larry Burkett

Faith in Christ is the victory that overcomes not only the world but also every engrained sin of the flesh.

Jim Cymbala

As a child of God, you are no longer a slave to sin.

Kay Arthur

When it comes to sin, commit to not commit!

Anonymous

TODAY'S INTEGRITY BUILDER

When given the opportunity to "try" something that might turn into a bad habit, don't. The slippery slope might be steeper than it looks.

TODAY'S PRAYER

Dear Lord, give me the wisdom and the strength to stay far away from the temptations of this world. Keep me mindful that there are no "little" sins, and that the only lasting peace comes not from the world, but from you. Amen

DAY 28

GENEROSITY BUILDS CHARACTER

Freely you have received, freely give.
Matthew 10:8 NKJV

Every time you give generously to those who need your help, you're strengthening your character. So, if you're looking for a surefire way to improve the quality of your life, here it is: be more generous.

The thread of generosity is woven—completely and inextricably—into the very fabric of Christ's teachings. As He sent His disciples out to heal the sick and spread God's message of salvation, Jesus offered this guiding principle: "Freely you have received, freely give" (Matthew 10:8 NIV). The principle still applies. If we are to be disciples of Christ, we must give freely of our time, our possessions, and our love.

In 2 Corinthians 9, Paul reminds us that when we sow the seeds of generosity, we reap bountiful rewards in accordance with God's plan for our lives. Thus, we are instructed to give cheerfully and without reservation: "But this I say: He who sows sparingly will also reap sparingly, and he who sows bountifully will also reap bountifully. So let each one give as he purposes in his heart, not grudgingly or of necessity; for God loves a cheerful giver" (vv. 6-7 NKJV).

Today, you may feel the urge to hoard your blessings. Don't do it. Instead, give generously to those less fortunate than you. Find a need and fill it. Lend a helping hand and share a word of kindness. It's the godly thing to do—and it's the best way to live.

Let us give according to our incomes,
lest God make our incomes match our gifts.

—

Peter Marshall

Nothing is really ours until we share it.

C. S. Lewis

If you want to be truly happy, you won't find it on an endless quest for more stuff. You'll find it in receiving God's generosity and in passing that generosity along.

Bill Hybels

We are never more like God than when we give.

Charles Swindoll

Generosity is changing one's focus from self to others.

John Maxwell

God does not supply money to satisfy our every whim and desire. His promise is to meet our needs and provide an abundance so that we can help other people.

Larry Burkett

TODAY'S INTEGRITY BUILDER

Would you like to be a little happier? Try sharing a few more of the blessings that God has bestowed upon you. In other words, if you want to be happy, be generous. And if you want to be unhappy, be greedy. And if you're not sure about the best way to give, pray about it.

As each one has received a gift, minister it to one another, as good stewards of the manifold grace of God.

1 Peter 4:10 NKJV

But this I say: He who sows sparingly will also reap sparingly, and he who sows bountifully will also reap bountifully. So let each one give as he purposes in his heart, not grudgingly or of necessity; for God loves a cheerful giver.

2 Corinthians 9:6-7 NKJV

In every way I've shown you that by laboring like this, it is necessary to help the weak and to keep in mind the words of the Lord Jesus, for He said, "It is more blessed to give than to receive."

Acts 20:35 Holman CSB

Cast your bread upon the waters, for you will find it after many days.

Ecclesiastes 11:1 NKJV

TODAY'S PRAYER

Lord, make me a generous and cheerful Christian. Let me be kind to those who need my encouragement, and let me share with those who need my help, today and every day. Amen

PATIENCE BUILDS CHARACTER

Be gentle to everyone, able to teach, and patient.
2 Timothy 2:23 Holman CSB

The dictionary defines the word *patience* as "the ability to be calm, tolerant, and understanding." If that describes you, you can skip the rest of this page. But, if you're like most of us, you'd better keep reading.

For most of us, patience is a hard thing to master. Why? Because we have lots of things we want, and we know precisely when we want them: NOW (if not sooner). But our Father in heaven has other ideas; the Bible teaches that we must learn to wait patiently for the things that God has in store for us, even when waiting is difficult.

We live in an imperfect world inhabited by imperfect people. Sometimes, we inherit troubles from others, and sometimes we create troubles for ourselves. On other occasions, we see other people "moving ahead" in the world, and we want to move ahead with them. So we become impatient with ourselves, with our circumstances, and even with our Creator.

Psalm 37:7 commands us to "rest in the Lord, and wait patiently for Him" (NKJV). But, for most of us, waiting patiently for Him is hard. We are fallible human beings who seek solutions to our problems today, not tomorrow. Still, God instructs us to wait patiently for His plans to unfold, and that's exactly what we should do.

Sometimes, patience is the price we pay for being responsible adults, and that's as it should be. After all, think how patient our Heavenly Father has been with us. So the next time you find yourself drumming your fingers as you wait for a quick resolution to the challenges of everyday living, take a deep breath and ask God for patience. Remember that patience builds character . . . and the best moment to start building is this one.

By his wisdom, he orders his delays
so that they prove to be far better than our hurries.

—

C. H. Spurgeon

You can't step in front of God and not get in trouble. When He says, "Go three steps," don't go four.

Charles Stanley

In all negotiations of difficulties, a man may not look to sow and reap at once. He must prepare his business and so ripen it by degrees.

Francis Bacon

As we wait on God, He helps us use the winds of adversity to soar above our problems. As the Bible says, "Those who wait on the LORD . . . shall mount up with wings like eagles."

Billy Graham

TODAY'S INTEGRITY BUILDER

The best things in life seldom happen overnight; they usually take time. Henry Blackaby writes, "The grass that is here today and gone tomorrow does not require much time to mature. A big oak tree that lasts for generations requires much more time to grow and mature. God is concerned about your life through eternity. Allow Him to take all the time He needs to shape you for His purposes. Larger assignments will require longer periods of preparation." How true.

Patience is better than power, and controlling one's temper, than capturing a city.

Proverbs 16:32 Holman CSB

But if we hope for what we do not see, we eagerly wait for it with patience.

Romans 8:25 Holman CSB

The Lord is good to those who wait for Him, to the person who seeks Him.

Lamentations 3:25 Holman CSB

Wait on the LORD; be of good courage, and He shall strengthen your heart; wait, I say, on the LORD!

Psalm 27:14 NKJV

TODAY'S PRAYER

Heavenly Father, let me wait quietly for You. Let me live according to Your plan and according to Your timetable. When I am hurried, slow me down. When I become impatient with others, give me empathy. Today, I want to be a patient Christian, Dear Lord, as I trust in You and in Your master plan. Amen

DAY 30

YOU AND YOUR CONSCIENCE

Blessed is the man who does not condemn himself.
Romans 14:22 Holman CSB

Billy Graham correctly observed, "Most of us follow our conscience as we follow a wheelbarrow. We push it in front of us in the direction we want to go." To do so, of course, is a profound mistake. Yet all of us, on occasion, have failed to listen to the voice that God planted in our hearts, and all of us have suffered the consequences of our choices.

God gave each of us a conscience for a very good reason: to listen to it. Wise believers make it a practice to listen carefully to that quiet internal voice. Count yourself among that number. When your conscience speaks, listen and learn. In all likelihood, God is trying to get His message through. And in all likelihood, it is a message that you desperately need to hear.

Few things in life torment us more than a guilty conscience. And, few things in life provide more contentment than the knowledge that we are obeying God's commandments. A clear conscience is one of the rewards we earn when we obey God's Word and follow His will. When we follow God's will and accept His gift of salvation, our earthly rewards are never-ceasing, and our heavenly rewards are everlasting.

To go against one's conscience is neither safe nor right. Here I stand. I cannot do otherwise.

Martin Luther

Guilt is a healthy regret for telling God one thing and doing another.

Max Lucado

God considers a pure conscience a very valuable thing— one that keeps our faith on a steady course.

Charles Stanley

TODAY'S INTEGRITY BUILDER

Today, remember this: the more important the decision . . . the more carefully you should listen to your conscience.

Now the goal of our instruction is love from a pure heart, a good conscience, and a sincere faith.

1 Timothy 1:5 Holman CSB

If then you were raised with Christ, seek those things which are above, where Christ is, sitting at the right hand of God. Set your mind on things above, not on things on the earth.

Colossians 3:1-2 NKJV

And do not be conformed to this world, but be transformed by the renewing of your mind, that you may prove what is that good and acceptable and perfect will of God.

Romans 12:2 NKJV

For indeed, the kingdom of God is within you.

Luke 17:21 NKJV

TODAY'S PRAYER

Dear Lord, You speak to me through the gift of Your Holy Word. And, Father, You speak to me through that still small voice that tells me right from wrong. Let me follow Your way, Lord, and, in these quiet moments, show me Your plan for this day, that I might serve You. Amen

DAY 31

WORSHIP BUILDS CHARACTER

Make a joyful shout to the Lord, all you lands!
Serve the Lord with gladness;
Come before His presence with singing.
Psalm 100:1-2 NKJV

Why do you attend church? Is it because of your sincere desire to worship and to praise God? Hopefully so. Yet far too many Christians attend worship services because they believe they are "supposed to go to church" or because they feel "pressured" to attend. Still others go to church for "social" reasons. But make no mistake: the best reason to attend church is out of a sincere desire to please God, to praise God, to experience God, and to discern God's will for your life.

Some people may tell you that they don't engage in worship. Don't believe them. All of mankind is engaged in worship. The question is not whether we worship, but what we worship. Wise men choose to worship God. When they do, they are blessed with a plentiful harvest of joy, peace, and abundance. Other people choose to distance themselves from God by foolishly worshiping things that are intended to bring personal gratification but not spiritual gratification. Such choices often have tragic consequences.

If we place our love for material possessions or social status above our love for God—or if we yield to the countless temptations of this world—we find ourselves engaged in a struggle between good and evil, a clash between God and Satan. Our responses to these struggles have implications that echo throughout our families and throughout our communities.

How can we ensure that we cast our lot with God? We do so, in part, by the character-building practice of regular, purposeful worship in the company of fellow believers. When we worship God faithfully and fervently, we are blessed. When we fail to worship God, for whatever reason, we forfeit the spiritual gifts that might otherwise be ours.

We must worship our Heavenly Father, not just with our words, but also with our deeds. We must honor Him, praise Him, and obey Him. As we seek to find purpose and meaning for our lives, we must first seek His purpose and His will. For believers, God comes first. Always first.

God asks that we worship Him with our concentrated minds as well as with our wills and emotions. A divided and scattered mind is not effective.

Catherine Marshall

When God is at the center of your life, you worship. When he's not, you worry.

Rick Warren

We're here to be worshipers first and workers only second. The work done by a worshiper will have eternity in it.

A. W. Tozer

In commanding us to glorify Him, God is inviting us to enjoy Him.

C. S. Lewis

Worship is your spirit responding to God's Spirit.

Rick Warren

TODAY'S INTEGRITY BUILDER

Worship reminds you of the awesome power of God. So worship Him daily, and allow Him to work through you every day of the week (not just on Sunday). The best way to worship God is to worship Him sincerely and often.

But an hour is coming, and is now here, when the true worshipers will worship the Father in spirit and truth. Yes, the Father wants such people to worship Him. God is Spirit, and those who worship Him must worship in spirit and truth.

John 4:23-24 Holman CSB

If any man thirst, let him come unto me, and drink.

John 7:37 KJV

For it is written, "You shall worship the Lord your God, and Him only you shall serve."

Matthew 4:10 NKJV

But seek first the kingdom of God and His righteousness, and all these things shall be added to you.

Matthew 6:33 NKJV

TODAY'S PRAYER

Heavenly Father, let today and every day be a time of worship for me and my family. Let us worship You, not only with words, but also with deeds. In the quiet moments of the day, let us praise You and thank You for creating us, loving us, guiding us, and saving us. Amen

DAY 32

KINDNESS BUILDS CHARACTER

A kind man benefits himself,
but a cruel man brings disaster on himself.
Proverbs 11:17 Holman CSB

Kindness builds character just as surely as hatred destroys it. But kindness doesn't always come easy. When we are discouraged, tired, or afraid, we can scarcely summon the energy to utter a single kind word. But, God's commandment is clear: He intends that we make the conscious choice to treat others with kindness and respect, no matter our circumstances, no matter our emotions.

In the busyness and confusion of daily life, it is easy to lose focus, and it is easy to become frustrated. We are imperfect human beings struggling to manage our lives as best we can, but we often fall short. When we are distracted or disappointed, we may neglect to share a kind word or a kind deed. This oversight hurts others, but it hurts us most of all.

Today, slow yourself down and be alert for people who need your smile, your kind words, or your helping hand.

Make kindness a centerpiece of your dealings with others. They will be blessed, and you will be, too.

When you weave the thread of kindness into the very fabric of your life, you'll be strengthening your character, but that's not all. You'll also be giving glory to the One who gave His life for you. And as a believer, you must do no less.

When you extend hospitality to others,
you're not trying to impress people,
you're trying to reflect God to them.

—

Max Lucado

Be so preoccupied with good will that you haven't room for ill will.

E. Stanley Jones

Do all the good you can. By all the means you can. In all the ways you can. In all the places you can. At all the times you can. To all the people you can. As long as ever you can.

John Wesley

If we have the true love of God in our hearts, we will show it in our lives. We will not have to go up and down the earth proclaiming it. We will show it in everything we say or do.

D. L. Moody

When you launch an act of kindness out into the crosswinds of life, it will blow kindness back to you.

Dennis Swanberg

TODAY'S INTEGRITY BUILDER

As you plan for the day ahead, remember this: kind words cost nothing, but when they're spoken at the right time, they can be priceless.

And be kind and compassionate to one another, forgiving one another, just as God also forgave you in Christ.

Ephesians 4:32 Holman CSB

Carry one another's burdens; in this way you will fulfill the law of Christ.

Galatians 6:2 Holman CSB

Now finally, all of you should be like-minded and sympathetic, should love believers, and be compassionate and humble.

1 Peter 3:8 Holman CSB

And may the Lord make you increase and abound in love to one another and to all.

1 Thessalonians 3:12 NKJV

TODAY'S PRAYER

Help me, Lord, to see the needs of those around me. Today, let me show courtesy to those who cross my path. Today, let me spread kind words in honor of Your Son. Today, let forgiveness rule my heart. And every day, Lord, let my love for Christ be demonstrated through the acts of kindness that I offer to those who need the healing touch of the Master's hand. Amen

DAY 33

MAKING THE MOST OF MISTAKES

Instead, God has chosen the world's foolish things to shame the wise, and God has chosen the world's weak things to shame the strong.

1 Corinthians 1:27 Holman CSB

Everybody makes mistakes, and so will you. In fact, Winston Churchill once observed, "Success is going from failure to failure without loss of enthusiasm." What was good for Churchill is also good for you, too. You should expect to make mistakes—plenty of them—but you should not allow those missteps to rob you of the enthusiasm you need to fulfill God's plan for your life.

We are imperfect people living in an imperfect world; mistakes are simply part of the price we pay for being here. But, even though mistakes are an inevitable part of life's journey, repeated mistakes should not be. When we commit the inevitable blunders of life, we must correct them, learn from them, and pray for the wisdom not to repeat them. When we do, our mistakes become lessons, and our experiences become adventures in character-building.

When our shortcomings are made public, we may feel embarrassed or worse. We may presume (quite incorrectly) that "everybody" is concerned with gravity of our problem. And, as a consequence, we may feel the need to hide from our problems rather than confront them. To do so is wrong. Even when our pride is bruised, we must face up to our mistakes and seek to rise above them.

Have you made a king-sized blunder or two? Of course you have. But here's the big question: have you used your mistakes as stumbling blocks or stepping stones? The answer to this question will determine how well you perform in the workplace and in every other aspect of your life. So don't let the fear of past failures hold you back. Instead, do the character-building thing: own up to your mistakes and do your best to fix them. Remember: even if you've made a colossal blunder, God isn't finished with you yet—in fact, He's probably just getting started.

Father, take our mistakes
and turn them into opportunities.

—

Max Lucado

Truth will sooner come out of error than from confusion.

Francis Bacon

Lord, when we are wrong, make us willing to change; and when we are right, make us easy to live with.

Peter Marshall

I hope you don't mind me telling you all this. One can learn only by seeing one's mistakes.

C. S. Lewis

Very few things motivate us to give God our undivided attention like being faced with the negative consequences of our decisions.

Charles Stanley

There is nothing wrong with asking God's direction. But it is wrong to go our own way, then expect Him to bail us out.

Larry Burkett

TODAY'S INTEGRITY BUILDER

Fix it sooner rather than later: When you make a mistake, the time to make things better is now, not later! The sooner you address your problem, the better. If not now, when?

Therefore if anyone is in Christ, he is a new creature; the old things passed away; behold, new things have come.

2 Corinthians 5:17 Holman CSB

If we confess our sins, He is faithful and righteous to forgive us our sins and to cleanse us from all unrighteousness.

1 John 1:9 Holman CSB

Be gracious to me, God, according to Your faithful love; according to Your abundant compassion, blot out my rebellion. Wash away my guilt, and cleanse me from my sin.

Psalm 51:1-2 Holman CSB

I waited patiently for the Lord, and He turned to me and heard my cry for help. He brought me up from a desolate pit, out of the muddy clay, and set my feet on a rock, making my steps secure. He put a new song in my mouth, a hymn of praise to our God.

Psalm 40:1-3 Holman CSB

TODAY'S PRAYER

Dear Lord, there's a right way to do things and a wrong way to do things. When I do things that are wrong, help me be quick to ask for forgiveness . . . and quick to correct my mistakes. Amen

A LIFE OF INTEGRITY

*Better is the poor who walks in his integrity
than one who is perverse in his lips, and is a fool.*

Proverbs 19:1 NKJV

Charles Swindoll correctly observed, "Nothing speaks louder or more powerfully than a life of integrity." Godly men agree.

Integrity is built slowly over a lifetime. It is the sum of every right decision and every honest word. It is forged on the anvil of honorable work and polished by the twin virtues of honesty and fairness. Integrity is a precious thing—difficult to build but easy to tear down.

As believers in Christ, we must seek to live each day with discipline, honesty, and faith. When we do, at least two things happen: integrity becomes a habit, and God blesses us because of our obedience to Him.

Living a life of integrity isn't always the easiest way, but it is always the right way. God clearly intends that it should be our way, too.

It has been said that character is what we are when nobody is watching. How true. When we do things that we know aren't right, we try to hide them from our families and friends. But even if we successfully conceal our sins from the world, we can never conceal our sins from God.

If you sincerely wish to walk with your Creator, follow His commandments. When you do, your character will take care of itself . . . and you won't need to look over your shoulder to see who, besides God, is watching.

A little lie is like a little pregnancy.
It doesn't take long before everyone knows.

—

C. S. Lewis

Integrity is not a given factor in everyone's life. It is a result of self-discipline, inner trust, and a decision to be relentlessly honest in all situations in our lives.

John Maxwell

God doesn't expect you to be perfect, but he does insist on complete honesty.

Rick Warren

Integrity is a sign of maturity.

Charles Swindoll

There's nothing like the power of integrity. It is a characteristic so radiant, so steady, so consistent, so beautiful, that it makes a permanent picture in our minds.

Franklin Graham

Today's Integrity Builder

One of your greatest possessions is integrity . . . don't lose it. Billy Graham was right when he said: "Integrity is the glue that holds our way of life together. We must constantly strive to keep our integrity intact. When wealth is lost, nothing is lost; when health is lost, something is lost; when character is lost, all is lost."

I will cling to my righteousness and never let it go. My conscience will not accuse [me] as long as I live!

Job 27:6 Holman CSB

The one who lives with integrity lives securely, but whoever perverts his ways will be found out.

Proverbs 10:9 Holman CSB

The integrity of the upright will guide them.

Proverbs 11:3 NKJV

Mercy and truth preserve the king, and by lovingkindness he upholds his throne.

Proverbs 20:28 NKJV

TODAY'S PRAYER

Heavenly Father, You instruct Your children to seek truth and to live righteously. Help me always to live according to Your commandments. Sometimes, Lord, speaking the truth is difficult, but let me always speak truthfully and forthrightly. And, let me walk righteously and courageously so that others might see Your grace reflected in my words and my deeds. Amen

DAY 35

GOD GIVES US STRENGTH

Cast your burden on the Lord, and He will support you; He
will never allow the righteous to be shaken.

Psalm 55:22 Holman CSB

I t's a promise that is made over and over again in the
Bible: Whatever "it" is, God can handle it.

Life isn't always easy. Far from it! Sometimes,
life can seem like a long, tiring, character-building, fear-
provoking journey. But even when the storm clouds form
overhead, even during our darkest moments, we're protected by a loving Heavenly Father.

When we're worried, God can reassure us; when
we're sad, God can comfort us. When our hearts are broken, God is not just near; He is here. So we must lift our
thoughts and prayers to Him. When we do, He will answer
our prayers. Why? Because He is our shepherd, and He has
promised to protect us now and forever.

God's hand uplifts those who turn their hearts and
prayers to Him. Will you count yourself among that number? Will you accept God's peace and wear God's armor
against the temptations and distractions of our dangerous
world? If you do, you can live courageously and optimisti-

cally, knowing that even on the darkest days, you and your Heavenly Father can handle every challenge you face, today and forever.

The next time you're disappointed, don't panic. Don't give up. Just be patient and let God remind you he's still in control.

Max Lucado

The God we seek is a God who is intrinsically righteous and who will be so forever. With His example and His strength, we can share in that righteousness.

Bill Hybels

You may not know what you are going to do; you only know that God knows what He is going to do.

Oswald Chambers

TODAY'S INTEGRITY BUILDER

Today, think about ways that you can tap into God's strength: try prayer, worship, and praise, for starters.

He gives strength to the weary and strengthens the powerless.

Isaiah 40:29 Holman CSB

Finally, be strengthened by the Lord and by His vast strength.

Ephesians 6:10 Holman CSB

You, therefore, my child, be strong in the grace that is in Christ Jesus.

2 Timothy 2:1 Holman CSB

The Lord is my strength and my song; He has become my salvation.

Exodus 15:2 Holman CSB

TODAY'S PRAYER

Dear Lord, You rule over our world, and I will allow You to rule over my heart. I will obey Your commandments, I will study Your Word, and I will seek Your will for my life, today and every day of my life. Amen

DAY 36

HABITS BECOME CHARACTER

Do not be deceived:
"Evil company corrupts good habits."
1 Corinthians 15:33 NKJV

I t's an old saying and a true one: First, you make your habits, and then your habits make you. Some habits are character-builders, inevitably bringing you closer to God while other habits will lead you away from the path He has chosen for you. If you sincerely desire to improve your spiritual health, you must honestly examine the habits that make up the fabric of your day. And you must abandon those habits that are displeasing to God.

Perhaps you've tried to become a more disciplined person, but you're still falling back into your old habits. If so, don't get discouraged. Instead, you should become even more determined to evolve into the person God wants you to be.

If you trust God, and if you keep asking for His help, He can transform your life. If you sincerely ask Him to help you, the same God who created the universe will help you defeat the harmful habits that have heretofore defeated you. So, if at first you don't succeed, keep praying. God is listening, and He's ready to help you become a better person if you ask Him . . . so ask today.

You will never change your life until you change something you do daily.

John Maxwell

The simple fact is that if we sow a lifestyle that is in direct disobedience to God's reveled Word, we ultimately reap disaster.

Charles Swindoll

Since behaviors become habits, make them work with you and not against you.

E. Stanley Jones

TODAY'S INTEGRITY BUILDER

Target your most unhealthy habit first, and attack it with vigor. When it comes to defeating harmful habitual behaviors, you'll need focus, determination, more focus, and more determination.

Dear friend, I pray that you may prosper in every way and be in good health, just as your soul prospers.

3 John 1:2 Holman CSB

Therefore, brothers, by the mercies of God, I urge you to present your bodies as a living sacrifice, holy and pleasing to God; this is your spiritual worship.

Romans 12:1 Holman CSB

Don't you know that you are God's sanctuary and that the Spirit of God lives in you?

1 Corinthians 3:16 Holman CSB

Do you not know that your body is a sanctuary of the Holy Spirit who is in you, whom you have from God? You are not your own, for you were bought at a price; therefore glorify God in your body.

1 Corinthians 6:19-20 Holman CSB

TODAY'S PRAYER

Dear Lord, help me break bad habits and form good ones. And let my actions be pleasing to You, today and every day. Amen

DAY 37

LISTENING TO GUILT

*There is therefore now no condemnation to those who are in
Christ Jesus, who do not walk according to the flesh,
but according to the Spirit.*

Romans 8:1 NKJV

All of us have sinned. Sometimes our sins result from our own stubborn rebellion against God's commandments. Sometimes, we are swept up by events that encourage us to behave in ways that we later come to regret. And sometimes, even when our intentions are honorable, we make mistakes that have long-lasting consequences. When we look back at our actions with remorse, we may experience intense feelings of guilt. But God has an answer for the guilt that we feel. That answer, of course, is His forgiveness.

When we genuinely repent from our wrongdoings, and when we sincerely confess our sins, we are forgiven by our Heavenly Father. But sometimes, long after God has forgiven us, we may continue to withhold forgiveness from ourselves. Instead of accepting God's mercy and accepting our past, we may think long and hard—far too long and hard—about the things that "might have been," the things that "could have been," or the things that "should have been."

Are you troubled by feelings of guilt, even after you've received God's forgiveness? Are you still struggling with painful memories of mistakes you made long ago? Are you focused so intently on yesterday that your vision of today is clouded? If so you still have work to do—spiritual work. You should ask your Heavenly Father not for forgiveness (He granted that gift the very first time you asked Him!) but instead for acceptance and trust: acceptance of the past and trust in God's plan for your life.

If you find yourself plagued by feelings of guilt or shame, consult God's survival guide: His Holy Word. And as you do so, consider the following biblically-based tips for overcoming those feeling of guilt once and for all:

1. Stop doing the things that make you feel guilty: How can you expect not to feel guilty if you should feel guilty? (Acts 26:20) 2. Ask God for forgiveness. When you ask for it, He will give it. (1 John 1:9) 3. Ask forgiveness from the people you have harmed: This step is hard, but helpful. And even if the other folks cannot find it in their hearts to forgive you, you have the satisfaction of knowing you that you asked. (Proverbs 28:13) 4. Forgive yourself: if you're no longer misbehaving, it's the right thing to do. And today is the right day to do it. (Romans 14:22) 5. Become more diligent in your daily time of prayer and Bible study. A regular time of quiet reflection and prayer will

allow you to praise your Creator, to focus your thoughts, to remind yourself of His love, and to seek His guidance in matters great and small. (Isaiah 50:4-5) 6. Get busy making the world a better place. Now that God has forgiven you, it's time for you to show your gratitude by serving Him. (Matthew 23:11-12).

Prayer is essential when a believer is stuck in the pits of unresolved guilt.

Charles Stanley

What the devil loves is that vague cloud of unspecified guilt feeling or unspecified virtue by which he lures us into despair or presumption.

C. S. Lewis

Don't be bound by your guilt or your fears any longer, but realize that sin's penalty has already been paid by Christ completely and fully.

Billy Graham

TODAY'S INTEGRITY BUILDER

Feeling Guilty? Think about how you should act and then stop doing the things that make you feel that way.

Be diligent to present yourself approved to God, a worker who doesn't need to be ashamed, correctly teaching the word of truth.

2 Timothy 2:15 Holman CSB

Blessed is the man who does not condemn himself.

Romans 14:22 Holman CSB

So now, little children, remain in Him, so that when He appears we may have boldness and not be ashamed before Him at His coming.

1 John 2:28-29 Holman CSB

TODAY'S PRAYER

Dear Lord, thank You for the guilt that I feel when I disobey You. Help me confess my wrongdoings, help me accept Your forgiveness, and help me renew my passion to serve You. Amen

DAY 38

PERSEVERANCE BUILDS CHARACTER

For you need endurance, so that after you have done God's will, you may receive what was promised.

Hebrews 10:36 Holman CSB

As you continue to seek God's purpose for your life, you will undoubtedly experience your fair share of disappointments, detours, false starts, and failures. When you do, you're facing one of those inevitable tests of character. Don't become discouraged: God's not finished with you yet.

The old saying is as true today as it was when it was first spoken: "Life is a marathon, not a sprint." That's why wise travelers (like you) select a traveling companion who never tires and never falters. That partner, of course, is your Heavenly Father.

The next time you find your courage tested to the limit, remember that God is as near as your next breath, and remember that He offers strength and comfort to His children. He is your shield and your strength; He is your protector and your deliverer. Call upon Him in your hour of need and then be comforted. Whatever your challenge, whatever your trouble, God can help you persevere. And that's precisely what He'll do if you ask Him.

Perhaps you are in a hurry for God to help you resolve your difficulties. Perhaps you're anxious to earn the rewards that you feel you've already earned from life. Perhaps you're drumming your fingers, impatiently waiting for God to act. If so, be forewarned: God operates on His own timetable, not yours. Sometimes, God may answer your prayers with silence, and when He does, you must patiently persevere. In times of trouble, you must remain steadfast and trust in the merciful goodness of your Heavenly Father. Whatever your problem, He can manage it. Your job is to keep persevering until He does.

By perseverance the snail reached the ark.

—

C. H. Spurgeon

Jesus taught that perseverance is the essential element in prayer.

E. M. Bounds

Perseverance is more than endurance. It is endurance combined with absolute assurance and certainty that what we are looking for is going to happen.

Oswald Chambers

Battles are won in the trenches, in the grit and grime of courageous determination; they are won day by day in the arena of life.

Charles Swindoll

Let us not cease to do the utmost, that we may incessantly go forward in the way of the Lord; and let us not despair of the smallness of our accomplishments.

John Calvin

TODAY'S INTEGRITY BUILDER

Are you being tested? Call upon God. God can give you the strength to persevere, and that's exactly what you should ask Him to do.

Do you not know that the runners in a stadium all race, but only one receives the prize? Run in such a way that you may win. Now everyone who competes exercises self-control in everything. However, they do it to receive a perishable crown, but we an imperishable one.

1 Corinthians 9:24-25 Holman CSB

But as for you, be strong; don't be discouraged, for your work has a reward.

2 Chronicles 15:7 Holman CSB

So we must not get tired of doing good, for we will reap at the proper time if we don't give up.

Galatians 6:9 Holman CSB

TODAY'S PRAYER

Lord, when life is difficult, I am tempted to abandon hope in the future. But You are my God, and I can draw strength from You. Let me trust You, Father, in good times and in bad times. Let me persevere—even if my soul is troubled—and let me follow Your Son Jesus Christ this day and forever. Amen

DAY 39

BEYOND DISCOURAGEMENT

But as for you, be strong; don't be discouraged,
for your work has a reward.

2 Chronicles 15:7 Holman CSB

We Christians have many reasons to celebrate. God is in His heaven; Christ has risen, and we are the sheep of His flock. Yet sometimes, even the most devout believers may become discouraged. After all, we live in a world where expectations can be high and demands can be even higher.

When we fail to meet the expectations of others (or, for that matter, the expectations that we have set for ourselves), we may be tempted to abandon hope. But God has other plans. He knows exactly how He intends to use us. Our task is to remain faithful until He does.

When we are discouraged—on those cloudy days when our strength is sapped and our faith is shaken—there exists a source from which we can draw courage and wisdom. That source is God. When we seek to form a more intimate and dynamic relationship with our Creator, He renews our spirits and restores our souls. This promise is made clear Isaiah 40:

Have you not known? Have you not heard? The everlasting God, the Lord, the Creator of the ends of the earth, neither faints nor is weary. His understanding is unsearchable. He gives power to the weak, and to those who have no might He increases strength. Even the youths shall faint and be weary, and the young men shall utterly fall, but those who wait on the Lord shall renew their strength; they shall mount up with wings like eagles, they shall run and not be weary, they shall walk and not faint." (vv. 28-31 NKJV)

God offers us the strength to meet our challenges, and He offers us hope for the future. One way that He shares His message of hope is through the words of encouraging friends and family members.

As a faithful follower of the One from Galilee, you have every reason to be hopeful. So, if you have become discouraged with the direction of your day or your life, turn your thoughts and prayers to God—and associate with like-minded believers who do the same. And remember this: your Heavenly Father is a God of possibility, not negativity. He is your Shepherd; He never leaves your side; and the ultimate victory will be His. So how, then, can you ever stay discouraged for long?

Feelings of uselessness and hopelessness are not from God, but from the evil one, the devil, who wants to discourage you and thwart your effectiveness for the Lord.

Bill Bright

If I am asked how we are to get rid of discouragements, I can only say, as I have had to say of so many other wrong spiritual habits, we must give them up. It is never worth while to argue against discouragement. There is only one argument that can meet it, and that is the argument of God.

Hannah Whitall Smith

We should not be upset when unexpected and upsetting things happen. God, in his wisdom, means to make something of us which we have not yet attained, and He is dealing with us accordingly.

J. I. Packer

TODAY'S INTEGRITY BUILDER

If you're feeling discouraged, try to redirect your thoughts away from the troubles that plague you—focus, instead, upon the opportunities that surround you.

We are hard pressed on every side, yet not crushed; we are perplexed, but not in despair.

2 Corinthians 4:8 NKJV

I will say to God, my rock, "Why have You forgotten me? Why must I go about in sorrow because of the enemy's oppression?"

Psalm 42:9 Holman CSB

I will be with you when you pass through the waters . . . when you walk through the fire . . . the flame will not burn you. For I the Lord your God, the Holy One of Israel, and your Savior.

Isaiah 43:2-3 Holman CSB

Is anyone among you suffering? He should pray. Is anyone cheerful? He should sing praises.

James 5:13 Holman CSB

TODAY'S PRAYER

Heavenly Father, when I am discouraged, I will turn to You, and I will also turn to my Christian friends. I thank You, Father, for friends and family members who are willing to encourage me. I will acknowledge their encouragement, and I will share it. Amen

DAY 40

SPIRITUAL WARFARE

Therefore, submit to God. But resist the Devil,
and he will flee from you. Draw near to God,
and He will draw near to you. Cleanse your hands, sinners,
and purify your hearts, double-minded people!
James 4:7-8 Holman CSB

This world is God's creation, and it contains the wonderful fruits of His handiwork. But, the world also contains countless opportunities to stray from God's will. Temptations are everywhere, and the devil, it seems, never takes a day off. Our task, as believers, is to turn away from temptation and to place our lives squarely in the center of God's will.

In his letter to Jewish Christians, Peter offered a stern warning: "Your adversary, the devil, prowls around like a roaring lion, seeking someone to devour" (1 Peter 5:8 NASB). What was true in New Testament times is equally true in our own. Evil is indeed abroad in the world, and Satan continues to sow the seeds of destruction far and wide. In a very real sense, our world is at war: good versus evil, sin versus righteousness, hope versus suffering, praise versus apathy. As Christians, we must ensure that we place ourselves squarely on the right side of these conflicts: God's side. How can we do it? By thoughtfully studying God's Word, by regularly worshiping with fellow believers, and by guarding our hearts and minds against the subtle temptations of the enemy. When we do, we are protected.

There is but one good; that is God. Everything else is good when it looks to Him and bad when it turns from Him.

C. S. Lewis

God judged it better to bring good out of evil than to suffer no evil to exist.

St. Augustine

TODAY'S INTEGRITY BUILDER

It's out there, and it can hurt you. Evil does exist, and you will confront it. Prepare yourself by forming a genuine, life-changing relationship with God and His only begotten Son. There is darkness in this world, but God's light can overpower any darkness.

For everyone who practices wicked things hates the light and avoids it, so that his deeds may not be exposed. But anyone who lives by the truth comes to the light, so that his works may be shown to be accomplished by God.

John 3:20–21 Holman CSB

He replied, "Every plant that My heavenly Father didn't plant will be uprooted."

Matthew 15:13 Holman CSB

But the path of the just is like the shining sun, that shines ever brighter unto the perfect day. The way of the wicked is like darkness; they do not know what makes them stumble.

Proverbs 4:18-19 NKJV

TODAY'S PRAYER

Dear Lord, strengthen my walk with You. Evil can devour me, and it comes in so many disguises. Sometimes, Father, I need Your help to recognize right from wrong. Your presence in my life enables me to choose truth and to live a life that is pleasing to You. May I always live in Your presence, and may I walk with You today . . . and forever. Amen

DAY 41

WALKING WITH THE WISE BUILDS CHARACTER

So follow the way of good people,
and keep to the paths of the righteous.

Proverbs 2:20 Holman CSB

Do you wish to become wise? Then you must walk with people who, by their words and their presence, make you wiser. And, to the best of your ability, you must avoid those people who don't. That means that you must choose wise friends and mentors.

A savvy mentor can help you make character-building choices. And just as importantly, a thoughtful mentor can help you recognize and avoid the hidden big-time mistakes that can derail your day (or your life).

Wise mentors aren't really very hard to find if you look in the right places (but they're almost impossible to find if you look in the wrong places!). So today, as an exercise in character-building, select from your friends and family members a mentor whose judgment you trust. Then listen carefully to your mentor's advice and be willing to accept that advice even if accepting it requires effort, or pain, or both. Consider your mentor to be God's gift to you. Thank God for that gift, and use it.

The next best thing to being wise oneself is to live in a circle of those who are.

C. S. Lewis

God often keeps us on the path by guiding us through the counsel of friends and trusted spiritual advisors.

Bill Hybels

The effective mentor strives to help a man or woman discover what they can be in Christ and then holds them accountable to become that person.

Howard Hendricks

TODAY'S INTEGRITY BUILDER

Rely on the advice of trusted friends and mentors. Proverbs 1:5 makes it clear: "A wise man will hear and increase learning, and a man of understanding will attain wise counsel" (NKJV). Do you want to be wise? Seek counsel from wise people, starting today.

My brothers, if any among you strays from the truth, and someone turns him back, he should know that whoever turns a sinner from the error of his way will save his life from death and cover a multitude of sins.

James 5:19-20 Holman CSB

The way of a fool is right in his own eyes, but he who heeds counsel is wise.

Proverbs 12:15 NKJV

The one who walks with the wise will become wise, but a companion of fools will suffer harm.

Proverbs 13:20 Holman CSB

TODAY'S PRAYER

Dear Lord, thank You for family members, for friends, and for mentors. When I am troubled, let me turn to them for help, for guidance, for comfort, and for perspective. And Father, let me be a friend and mentor to others, so that my love for You may be reflected in my genuine concern for them. Amen

DAY 42

YOU'RE ACCOUNTABLE

But each person should examine his own work,
and then he will have a reason for boasting in himself alone,
and not in respect to someone else.
For each person will have to carry his own load.

Galatians 6:4-5 Holman CSB

We humans are masters at passing the buck. Why? Because passing the buck is easier than fixing, and criticizing others is so much easier than improving ourselves. So instead of solving our problems legitimately (by doing the work required to solve them) we are inclined to fret, to blame, and to criticize, while doing precious little else. When we do, our problems, quite predictably, remain unsolved.

Whether you like it or not, you (and only you) are accountable for your actions. But because you are human, you'll be sorely tempted to pass the blame. Avoid that temptation at all costs.

Problem-solving builds character. Every time you straighten your back and look squarely into the face of Old Man Trouble, you'll strengthen not only your backbone but also your spirit. So, instead of looking for someone to blame, look for something to fix, and then get busy fixing it. And as you consider your own situation, remember this: God has a way of helping those who help themselves, but He doesn't spend much time helping those who don't.

Generally speaking, accountability is a willingness to share our activities, conduct, and fulfillment of assigned responsibilities with others.

Charles Stanley

The Bible teaches that we are accountable to one another for our conduct and character.

Charles Stanley

Accountability is the glue that holds society together.

Rich DeVos

Today's Integrity Builder

It's easy to hold other people accountable, but real accountability begins with the person in the mirror. Think about one specific area of responsibility that is uniquely yours, and think about a specific step you can take today to better fulfill that responsibility.

Even a young man is known by his actions—by whether his behavior is pure and upright.

Proverbs 20:11 Holman CSB

So follow the way of good people, and keep to the paths of the righteous.

Proverbs 2:20 Holman CSB

Do what is right and good in the Lord's sight, so that you may prosper and so that you may enter and possess the good land the Lord your God swore to [give] your fathers.

Deuteronomy 6:18 Holman CSB

I, the Lord, examine the mind, I test the heart to give to each according to his way, according to what his actions deserve.

Jeremiah 17:10 Holman CSB

TODAY'S PRAYER

Dear Lord, give me the courage and the wisdom to accept responsibility for my actions. And keep me mindful, Father, that I must honor You with good thoughts, honest prayers, and responsible behavior, today and every day. Amen

SLOTH DESTROYS CHARACTER

Brothers, I do not consider myself to have taken hold of it.
But one thing I do: forgetting what is behind and reaching
forward to what is ahead, I pursue as my goal the prize
promised by God's heavenly call in Christ Jesus.

Philippians 3:13-14 Holman CSB

I f you'd like a surefire formula for tearing down your character, here it is: do everything you can to avoid doing an honest day's work. But if you'd like a proven formula for building character, do your work with vigor, dedication, and enthusiasm.

You've heard the advice since you were a child: "Give the boss an honest day's work for an honest day's pay." But sometimes, you'll going to be tempted to do otherwise. Why? For starters, no job is perfect—and that means that your job isn't perfect, either. So, from time to time, you'll probably become upset with your job, and it is during these times, when you're frustrated or upset, that you'll be tempted to gripe, to waste time, and to do little else. Avoid these temptations—they're self-destructive.

Even if you're planning on quitting your job tomorrow, give your boss a full day's work today. Otherwise, you'll be developing a very bad habit: the habit of giving less than 100%. It's a character-destroying trait, an easy habit to acquire and a difficult habit to break.

If you're looking for folks to waste time with, you can probably find them just about anywhere—including your workplace. But if you're looking for a meaningful life (not to mention a career that you love), make up your mind to be the kind of man whose work speaks (in glowing terms) for itself. When you do, you'll discover that when you give your best, you enjoy work the most.

The worst thing that laziness does
is rob a man of spiritual purpose.

—

Billy Graham

The only cure for laziness is to be filled with the life of God.

Oswald Chambers

He will clothe you in rags if you clothe yourself with idleness.

C. H. Spurgeon

As we make an offering of our work, we find the truth of a principle Jesus taught: Fulfillment is not a goal to achieve, but always the by-product of a sacrifice.

Elisabeth Elliot

Thank God every morning when you get up that you have something which must be done, whether you like it or not. Work breeds a hundred virtues that idleness never knows.

Charles Kingsley

TODAY'S INTEGRITY BUILDER

Feeling a little lazy? That means that you're not excited about your work. So here's your challenge: find work that's so much fun you can't wait to clock in. When you do, you'll discover that a really good job beats leisure (or retirement) hands down.

Whatever your hands find to do, do with [all] your strength.

Ecclesiastes 9:10 Holman CSB

He did it with all his heart. So he prospered.

2 Chronicles 31:21 NKJV

Don't work only while being watched, in order to please men, but as slaves of Christ, do God's will from your heart. Render service with a good attitude, as to the Lord and not to men.

Ephesians 6:6-7 Holman CSB

We must do the works of Him who sent Me while it is day. Night is coming when no one can work.

John 9:4 Holman CSB

TODAY'S PRAYER

Lord, I know that You desire a bountiful harvest for all Your children. But, You have instructed us that we must sow before we reap, not after. Help me, Lord, to sow the seeds of Your abundance everywhere I go. Let me be diligent in all my undertakings and give me patience to wait for Your harvest. In time, Lord, let me reap the harvest that is found in Your will for my life. Amen

DAY 44

TRUSTING HIS PROMISES

*Let us hold on to the confession of our hope without wavering,
for He who promised is faithful.*

Hebrews 10:23 Holman CSB

What do you expect from the day ahead? Are you willing to trust God completely or are you living beneath a cloud of doubt and fear? God's Word makes it clear: you should trust Him and His promises, and when you do, you can live courageously.

For thoughtful Christians, every day begins and ends with God's Son and God's promises. When we accept Christ into our hearts, God promises us the opportunity for earthly peace and spiritual abundance. But more importantly, God promises us the priceless gift of eternal life.

Sometimes, especially when we find ourselves caught in the inevitable entanglements of life, we fail to trust God completely.

Are you tired? Discouraged? Fearful? Be comforted and trust the promises that God has made to you. Are you worried or anxious? Be confident in God's power. Do you see a difficult future ahead? Be courageous and call upon God. He will protect you and then use you according to His purposes. Are you confused? Listen to the quiet voice of your Heavenly Father. He is not a God of confusion. Talk with Him; listen to Him; trust Him, and trust His promises. He is steadfast, and He is your Protector . . . forever.

We honor God by asking for great things when
they are a part of His promise.
We dishonor Him and cheat ourselves when
we ask for molehills
where He has promised mountains.

—

Vance Havner

There are four words I wish we would never forget, and they are, "God keeps his word."

Charles Swindoll

The stars may fall, but God's promises will stand and be fulfilled.

J. I. Packer

The promises of Scripture are not mere pious hopes or sanctified guesses. They are more than sentimental words to be printed on decorated cards for Sunday School children. They are eternal verities. They are true. There is no perhaps about them.

Peter Marshall

God's promises are overflowings from his great heart.

C. H. Spurgeon

Today's Integrity Builder

Do you really trust God's promises, or are you hedging your bets? Today, think about the role that God's Word plays in your life, and think about ways that you can worry less and trust God more.

For you need endurance, so that after you have done God's will, you may receive what was promised.

Hebrews 10:36 Holman CSB

Sustain me as You promised, and I will live; do not let me be ashamed of my hope.

Psalm 119:116 Holman CSB

God—His way is perfect; the word of the Lord is pure. He is a shield to all who take refuge in Him.

Psalm 18:30 Holman CSB

Because God wanted to show His unchangeable purpose even more clearly to the heirs of the promise, He guaranteed it with an oath, so that through two unchangeable things, in which it is impossible for God to lie, we who have fled for refuge might have strong encouragement to seize the hope set before us.

Hebrews 6:17-18 Holman CSB

TODAY'S PRAYER

Lord, Your Holy Word contains promises, and I will trust them. I will use the Bible as my guide, and I will trust You, Lord, to speak to me through Your Holy Spirit and through Your Holy Word, this day and forever. Amen

DAY 45

REAL TRANSFORMATION?
INNER TRANSFORMATION!

Therefore if anyone is in Christ, he is a new creature;
the old things passed away; behold, new things have come.
2 Corinthians 5:17 Holman CSB

H ave you invited God's Son to reign over your
heart and your life? If so, think for a moment
about the "old" you, the person you were before
you invited Christ into your heart. Now, think about the
"new" you, the person you have become since then. Is
there a difference between the "old" you and the "new and
improved" version? There should be! And that difference
should be noticeable not only to you but also to others.

Warren Wiersbe observed, "The greatest miracle of all
is the transformation of a lost sinner into a child of God."
And Oswald Chambers noted, "If the Spirit of God has
transformed you within, you will exhibit Divine characteristics in your life, not good human characteristics. God's
life in us expresses itself as God's life, not as a human life
trying to be godly."

When you invited Christ to reign over your heart,
you became a new creation through Him. This day offers

yet another opportunity to behave yourself like that new creation by serving your Creator and strengthening your character. When you do, God will guide your steps and bless your endeavors today and forever.

No man is ever the same after God has laid His hand upon him.

A. W. Tozer

God wants to change our lives—and He will, as we open our hearts to Him.

Billy Graham

Trusting Jesus Christ has changed me so completely that I scarcely know my former self.

C. H. Spurgeon

When I met Christ, I felt that I had swallowed sunshine.

E. Stanley Jones

TODAY'S INTEGRITY BUILDER

Today, remember this: a true conversion experience results in a life transformed by Christ and a commitment to following in His footsteps.

Jesus replied, "I assure you: Unless someone is born again, he cannot see the kingdom of God." "But how can anyone be born when he is old?" Nicodemus asked Him. "Can he enter his mother's womb a second time and be born?" Jesus answered, "I assure you: Unless someone is born of water and the Spirit, he cannot enter the kingdom of God."

John 3:3–5 Holman CSB

Then He called a child to Him and had him stand among them. "I assure you," He said, "unless you are converted and become like children, you will never enter the kingdom of heaven."

Matthew 18:2-3 Holman CSB

Therefore we were buried with Him by baptism into death, in order that, just as Christ was raised from the dead by the glory of the Father, so we too may walk in a new way of life.

Romans 6:4 Holman CSB

TODAY'S PRAYER

Lord, when I accepted Jesus as my personal Savior, You changed me forever and made me whole. Let me share Your Son's message with my friends, with my family, and with the world. You are a God of love, redemption, conversion, and salvation. I will praise You today and forever. Amen

MATERIALISM TEARS DOWN CHARACTER

Don't collect for yourselves treasures on earth, where moth and rust destroy and where thieves break in and steal. But collect for yourselves treasures in heaven, where neither moth nor rust destroys, and where thieves don't break in and steal. For where your treasure is, there your heart will be also.

Matthew 6:19-21 Holman CSB

I n our modern society, we need money to live. But as Christians, we must never make the acquisition of money the central focus of our lives. Money is a tool, but it should never overwhelm our sensibilities. The focus of life must be squarely on things spiritual, not things material.

Whenever we place our love for material possessions above our love for God—or when we yield to the countless other temptations of everyday living—we find ourselves engaged in a struggle between good and evil. Let us respond to this struggle by freeing ourselves from that subtle yet powerful temptation: the temptation to love the world more than we love God.

Whenever we become absorbed with the acquisition of things, complications arise. Each new acquisition costs money or time, often both. To further complicate matters, many items can be purchased, not with real money, but with something much more insidious: debt. Debt—especially consumer debt used to purchase depreciating assets—is a modern-day form of indentured servitude.

If you're looking for a sure-fire, time-tested way to simplify your life and thereby improve your world, learn to control your possessions before they control you. Purchase only those things that make a significant contribution to your well-being and the well-being of your family. Never spend more than you make. Understand the folly in buying consumer goods on credit. Never use credit cards as a way of financing your lifestyle.

Ask yourself this simple question: "Do I own my possessions, or do they own me?" If you don't like the answer you receive, make an iron-clad promise to stop acquiring and start divesting. As you simplify your life, you'll be amazed at the things you can do without. You'll be pleasantly surprised at the sense of satisfaction that accompanies your new-found moderation. And you'll understand first-hand that when it comes to material possessions, less truly is more.

So, if you find yourself wrapped up in the concerns of the material world, it's time to reorder your priorities by turning your thoughts and your prayers to more important matters. And, it's time to begin storing up riches that will endure throughout eternity: the spiritual kind.

When possessions become our god, we become materialistic and greedy . . . and we forfeit our contentment and our joy.

Charles Swindoll

He is no fool who gives what he cannot keep to gain what he cannot lose.

Jim Elliot

Here's a simple test: If you can see it, it's not going to last. The things that last are the things you cannot see.

Dennis Swanberg

TODAY'S INTEGRITY BUILDER

Materialism Made Simple: The world wants you to believe that "money and stuff" can buy happiness. Don't believe it! Genuine happiness comes not from money, but from the things that money can't buy—starting, of course, with your relationship to God and His only begotten Son.

Do not love the world or the things in the world. If anyone loves the world, the love of the Father is not in him.

1 John 2:15 NKJV

He who trusts in his riches will fall, but the righteous will flourish . . . .

Proverbs 11:28 NKJV

For what will it profit a man if he gains the whole world, and loses his own soul? Or what will a man give in exchange for his soul?

Mark 8:36-37 NKJV

For where your treasure is, there your heart will be also.

Luke 12:34 NKJV

TODAY'S PRAYER

Lord, my greatest possession is my relationship with You through Jesus Christ. You have promised that, when I first seek Your kingdom and Your righteousness, You will give me whatever I need. Let me trust You completely, Lord, for my needs, both material and spiritual, this day and always. Amen

TAKING TIME
TO PRAISE GOD

*I will thank the Lord with all my heart; I will declare all Your
wonderful works. I will rejoice and boast about You;
I will sing about Your name, Most High.*

Psalm 9:1-2 Holman CSB

I f you'd like to strengthen your character, try spending
more time praising God. And when, by the way, is the
best time to praise God? In church? Before dinner is
served? When we tuck little children into bed? None of
the above. The best time to praise God is all day, every
day, to the greatest extent we can, with thanksgiving in
our hearts.

Too many of us, even well-intentioned believers, tend
to "compartmentalize" our waking hours into a few familiar categories: work, rest, play, family time, and worship.
To do so is a mistake. Worship and praise should be woven
into the fabric of everything we do; it should never be rel-
egated to a weekly three-hour visit to church on Sunday
morning.

Mrs. Charles E. Cowman, the author of the classic devotional text, *Streams in the Desert*, wrote, "Two wings are

necessary to lift our souls toward God: prayer and praise. Prayer asks. Praise accepts the answer." Today, find a little more time to lift your concerns to God in prayer, and praise Him for all that He has done. He's listening . . . and He wants to hear from you.

Be not afraid of saying too much in the praises of God; all the danger is of saying too little.

Matthew Henry

The Bible instructs—and experience teaches—that praising God results in our burdens being lifted and our joys being multiplied.

Jim Gallery

When there is peace in the heart, there will be praise on the lips.

Warren Wiersbe

TODAY'S INTEGRITY BUILDER

Remember that it always pays to praise your Creator. That's why thoughtful believers (like you) make it a habit to carve out quiet moments throughout the day to praise God.

Praise the Lord! Oh, give thanks to the Lord, for He is good! For His mercy endures forever.

Psalm 106:1 NKJV

In everything give thanks; for this is the will of God in Christ Jesus for you.

2 Thessalonians 5:18 NKJV

From the rising of the sun to its going down the Lord's name is to be praised.

Psalm 113:3 NKJV

But I will hope continually, and will praise You yet more and more.

Psalm 71:14 NKJV

TODAY'S PRAYER

Dear Lord, make me a man who gives constant praise to You. And, let me share the joyous news of Jesus Christ with a world that needs His transformation and His salvation. Amen

DAY 48

SOCIETY'S TREASURES

If you were of the world, the world would love you as its own. However, because you are not of the world, but I have chosen you out of the world, this is why the world hates you.

John 15:19 Holman CSB

All of mankind is engaged in a colossal, worldwide treasure hunt. Some people seek treasure from earthly sources, treasures such as material wealth or public acclaim; others seek God's treasures by making Him the cornerstone of their lives.

What kind of treasure hunter are you? Are you one of those men who has become so caught up in the demands of everyday living that you sometimes allow the search for worldly treasures to become your primary focus? If so, it's time to reorganize your daily to-do list by placing God in His rightful place: first place. Don't allow anyone or anything to separate you from your Heavenly Father and His only begotten Son.

The world's treasures are difficult to find and difficult to keep; God's treasures are ever-present and everlasting. Which treasures, then, will you claim as your own?

Because the world is deceptive, it is dangerous. The world can even deceive God's own people and lead them into trouble.

Warren Wiersbe

Christians don't fail to live as they should because they are in the world; they fail because the world has gotten into them.

Billy Graham

Our joy ends where love of the world begins.

C. H. Spurgeon

TODAY'S INTEGRITY BUILDER

If you're determined to be a faithful follower of the One from Galilee, you must make certain that you focus on His values, not society's values (and by the way, those two sets of values are almost never the same).

TODAY'S PRAYER

Lord, this world is a crazy place, and I have countless opportunities to stray from Your will. Help me to turn from evil, Father, as I keep Christ in my heart, today and every day. Amen

SEEKING GOD'S PLANS

"For I know the plans I have for you"—[this is] the Lord's declaration—"plans for [your] welfare, not for disaster, to give you a future and a hope."

Jeremiah 29:11 Holman CSB

"Why did God put me here?" It's a simple question to ask and, at times, a very complicated question to answer.

As you seek to discover (or perhaps, to rediscover) God's plan for your life, you should start by remembering this: You are here because God put you here, and He did so for a very good reason: His reason.

At times, you may be confident that you are doing God's will. But on other occasions, you may be uncertain about the direction that your life should take. At times, you may wander aimlessly in a wilderness of your own making. And sometimes, you may struggle mightily against God in a vain effort to find success and happiness through your own means, not His. But wherever you find yourself—whether on the mountaintops, in the valleys, or at the crossroads of life—you may be assured that God is there . . . and you may be assured that He has a plan.

If you manage to align yourself with God's plan for your life, you will be energized, you will be enthused, and you will be blessed. That's why you should strive mightily to understand what it is that God wants you to do. But how can you know precisely what God's intentions are? The answer, of course, is that even the most well-intentioned believers face periods of uncertainty and doubt about the direction of their lives. So, too, will you.

When you arrive at one of life's inevitable crossroads, that's the moment when you should turn your thoughts and prayers toward God. When you do, He will make Himself known to you in a time and manner of His choosing. When you discover God's plan for your life, you will experience abundance, peace, joy, and power—God's power.

And that's the only kind of power that really matters.

One of the wonderful things about being a Christian is the knowledge that God has a plan for our lives.

—

Warren Wiersbe

If God declares what it means to be human, then our lives are not the meaningless collections of unrelated events they so often appear to be.

Stanley Grenz

God will not permit any troubles to come upon us unless He has a specific plan by which great blessing can come out of the difficulty.

Peter Marshall

A saint's life is in the hands of God just as a bow and arrow are in the hands of an archer. God is aiming at something the saint cannot see.

Oswald Chambers

In God's plan, God is the standard for perfection. We don't compare ourselves to others; they are just as fouled up as we are. The goal is to be like him; anything less is inadequate.

Max Lucado

TODAY'S INTEGRITY BUILDER

God has a wonderful plan for your life. And the time to start looking for that plan—and living it—is now. And remember—discovering God's plan begins with prayer, but it doesn't end there. You've also got to work at it.

A man's heart plans his way, but the Lord directs his steps.

Proverbs 16:9 NKJV

We know that all things work together for the good of those who love God: those who are called according to His purpose.

Romans 8:28 Holman CSB

But as for you, you meant evil against me; but God meant it for good, in order to bring it about as it is this day, to save many people alive.

Genesis 50:20 NKJV

Teach me to do Your will, for You are my God. May Your gracious Spirit lead me on level ground.

Psalm 143:10 Holman CSB

TODAY'S PRAYER

Dear Lord, I will earnestly seek Your will for my life. You have a plan for me that I can never fully understand. But You understand. And I will trust You today, tomorrow, and forever. Amen

DAY 50

MONEY: TOOL OR MASTER?

For the love of money is a root of all kinds of evil, and by
craving it, some have wandered away from the faith and
pierced themselves with many pains.

1 Timothy 6:10 Holman CSB

Here's a scary thought: the content of your character is demonstrated by the way you choose to spend money. If you spend money wisely, and if you give God His fair share, then you're doing just fine. But if you're up to your eyeballs in debt, and if "shop till you drop" is your unofficial motto, it's time to retire the credit cards and rearrange your priorities.

Our society is in love with money and the things that money can buy. God is not. God cares about people, not possessions, and so must we. We must, to the best of our abilities, love our neighbors as ourselves, and we must, to the best of our abilities, resist the mighty temptation to place possessions ahead of people.

Money, in and of itself, is not evil; worshipping money is. So today, as you prioritize matters of importance for you and yours, remember that God is almighty, but the dollar is not.

Are you choosing to make money your master? If so, it's time to turn your thoughts and your prayers to more important matters. And, it's time to begin storing up riches that will endure throughout eternity: the spiritual kind.

Servants of God are always more concerned about ministry than money.

Rick Warren

Your priorities, passions, goals, and fears are shown clearly in the flow of your money.

Dave Ramsey

When I have any money, I get rid of it as quickly as possible, lest it find a way into my heart.

John Wesley

TODAY'S INTEGRITY BUILDER

Put God where He belongs—first: Any relationship that doesn't honor God is a relationship that is destined for problems—and that includes your relationship with money. So spend (and save) accordingly.

The borrower is a slave to the lender.

Proverbs 22:7 Holman CSB

Based on the gift they have received, everyone should use it to serve others, as good managers of the varied grace of God.

1 Peter 4:10 Holman CSB

Your life should be free from the love of money. Be satisfied with what you have, for He Himself has said, I will never leave you or forsake you.

Hebrews 13:5 Holman CSB

No one can be a slave of two masters, since either he will hate one and love the other, or be devoted to one and despise the other. You cannot be slaves of God and of money.

Matthew 6:24 Holman CSB

TODAY'S PRAYER

Dear Lord, help make me a responsible steward of my financial resources. Let me trust Your Holy Word, and let me use my tithe for the support of Your church and for the eternal glory of Your Son. Amen

BEYOND EXCUSES

Let us walk with decency, as in the daylight:
not in carousing and drunkenness.

Romans 13:13 Holman CSB

All too often we are quick to proclaim ourselves "victims," and we refuse to take responsibility for our actions. So we make excuses, excuses, and more excuses—with predictably poor results.

We live in a world where excuses are everywhere. And it's precisely because excuses are so numerous that they are also so ineffective. When we hear the words, "I'm sorry but . . . ," most of us know exactly what is to follow: the excuse. The dog ate the homework. Traffic was terrible. It's the company's fault. The boss is to blame. The equipment is broken. We're out of that. And so forth, and so on.

Because we humans are such creative excuse-makers, all of the really good excuses have already been taken. In fact, the high-quality excuses have been used, re-used, over-used, and abused. That's why excuses don't work— we've heard them all before.

So, if you're wasting your time trying to portray your-self as a victim (and weakening your character in the process), or if you're trying to concoct a new and improved excuse, don't bother. Excuses don't work, and while you're inventing them, neither do you.

Rationalization: It's what we do when
we substitute false explanations for true reasons,
when we cloud our actual motives with
a smoke screen of nice-sounding excuses.

—

Charles Swindoll

Replace your excuses with fresh determination.

Charles Swindoll

If you're looking for an excuse, you probably won't have much trouble finding it.

Criswell Freeman

An excuse is only the skin of a reason stuffed with a lie.

Vance Havner

TODAY'S INTEGRITY BUILDER

Today, think of something important that you've been putting off. Then think of the excuses you've used to avoid that responsibility. Finally, ask yourself what you can do today to finish the work you've been avoiding.

TODAY'S PRAYER

Heavenly Father, how easy it is to make excuses. But, I want to be a man who accomplishes important work for You. Help me, Father, to strive for excellence, not excuses. Amen

EMOTIONS: WHO'S IN CHARGE OF YOURS?

*For this very reason, make every effort to supplement
your faith with goodness, goodness with knowledge,
knowledge with self-control, self-control with endurance,
endurance with godliness.*

2 Peter 1:5-6 Holman CSB

Hebrews 10:38 teaches us that, "The just shall live by faith." Yet sometimes, despite our best intentions, negative feelings can rob us of the peace and abundance that would otherwise be ours through Christ. When anger or anxiety separates us from the spiritual blessings that God has in store, we must rethink our priorities and renew our faith. And we must place faith above feelings. Human emotions are highly variable, decidedly unpredictable, and often unreliable. Our emotions are like the weather, only far more fickle. So we must learn to live by faith, not by the ups and downs of our own emotional roller coasters.

Sometime during this day, you will probably be gripped by a strong negative emotion. Distrust it. Reign it in. Test it. And turn it over to God. Your emotions will inevitably change; God will not. So trust Him completely as you watch your feelings slowly evaporate into thin air—which, of course, they will.

Don't bother much about your feelings.
When they are humble, loving, brave,
give thanks for them; when they are conceited, selfish,
cowardly, ask to have them altered. In neither case are
they you, but only a thing that happens to you.
What matters is your intentions and your behavior.

—

C. S. Lewis

If you desire to improve your physical well-being and your emotional outlook, increasing your faith can help you.

John Maxwell

I do not need to feel good or be ecstatic in order to be in the center of God's will.

Bill Bright

TODAY'S INTEGRITY BUILDER

Remember: Your life shouldn't be ruled by your emotions— your life should be ruled by God. So if you think you've lost control over your emotions, don't make big decisions, don't strike out against anybody, and don't speak out in anger. Count to ten (or more) and take "time out" from your situation until you calm down.

TODAY'S PRAYER

Heavenly Father, You are my strength and my refuge. As I journey through this day, I will encounter events that cause me emotional distress. Lord, when I am troubled, let me turn to You. Keep me steady, Lord, and in those difficult moments, renew a right spirit inside my heart. Amen

THE CHARACTER-BUILDING PATH: FOLLOWING HIS FOOTSTEPS

"Follow Me," Jesus told them,
"and I will make you into fishers of men!"
Immediately they left their nets and followed Him.
Mark 1:17-18 Holman CSB

Jesus walks with you. Are you walking with Him? Hopefully, you will choose to walk with Him today and every day of your life.

Jesus loved you so much that He endured unspeakable humiliation and suffering for you. How will you respond to Christ's sacrifice? Will you take up His cross and follow Him (Luke 9:23), or will you choose another path? When you place your hopes squarely at the foot of the cross, when you place Jesus squarely at the center of your life, you will be blessed.

The old familiar hymn begins, "What a friend we have in Jesus . . . ." No truer words were ever penned. Jesus is the sovereign Friend and ultimate Savior of mankind. Christ showed enduring love for His believers by willingly sacrificing His own life so that we might have eternal life. Now, it is our turn to become His friend.

Let us love our Savior, let us praise Him, and let us share His message of salvation with the world. When we do, we demonstrate that our acquaintance with the Master is not a passing fancy, but is, instead, the cornerstone and the touchstone of our lives.

The heaviest end of the cross lies ever on His shoulders. If He bids us carry a burden, He carries it also.

—

C. H. Spurgeon

Imagine the spiritual strength the disciples drew from walking hundreds of miles with Jesus . . . 3 John 4.

John Maxwell

Our responsibility is to feed from Him, to stay close to Him, to follow Him—because sheep easily go astray—so that we eternally experience the protection and companionship of our Great Shepherd the Lord Jesus Christ.

Franklin Graham

Look for yourself, and you will find in the long run only hatred, loneliness, despair, rage, ruin and decay. But look for Christ, and you will find Him, and with Him everything else thrown in.

C. S. Lewis

A disciple is a follower of Christ. That means you take on His priorities as your own. His agenda becomes your agenda. His mission becomes your mission.

Charles Stanley

TODAY'S INTEGRITY BUILDER

Following Christ is a matter of obedience. If you want to be a little more like Jesus . . . learn about His teachings, follow in His footsteps, and obey His commandments.

Then He said to them all, "If anyone wants to come with Me, he must deny himself, take up his cross daily, and follow Me."

Luke 9:23 Holman CSB

For I have given you an example that you also should do just as I have done for you.

John 13:15 Holman CSB

No one can be a slave of two masters, since either he will hate one and love the other, or be devoted to one and despise the other. You cannot be slaves of God and of money.

Matthew 6:24 Holman CSB

Anyone finding his life will lose it, and anyone losing his life because of Me will find it.

Matthew 10:39 Holman CSB

TODAY'S PRAYER

Dear Lord, help me become the man I can be and should be. Guide me along a path of Your choosing, and let me follow in the footsteps of Your Son, today and every day. Amen

TOO FRIENDLY
WITH THE WORLD?

Let no one deceive himself. If anyone among you
seems to be wise in this age, let him become
a fool that he may become wise. For the wisdom of this world
is foolishness with God. For it is written,
"He catches the wise in their own craftiness."

1 Corinthians 3:18–19 NKJV

We live in the world, but we should not worship it—yet at every turn, or so it seems, we are tempted to do otherwise. As Warren Wiersbe correctly observed, "Because the world is deceptive, it is dangerous."

The 21st-century world in which we live is a noisy, distracting place, a place that offers countless temptations and dangers. The world seems to cry, "Worship me with your time, your money, your energy, your thoughts, and your life!" But if we are wise, we won't fall prey to that temptation.

If you wish to build your character day-by-day, you must distance yourself, at least in part, from the temptations and distractions of modern-day society. But distancing yourself isn't easy, especially when so many societal forces are struggling to capture your attention, your participation, and your money.

C. S. Lewis said, "Aim at heaven and you will get earth thrown in; aim at earth and you will get neither." That's good advice. You're likely to hit what you aim at, so aim high . . . aim at heaven. When you do, you'll be strengthening your character as you improve every aspect of your life. And God will demonstrate His approval as He showers you with more spiritual blessings than you can count.

There is no hell on earth like
horizontal living without God.

—

Charles Swindoll

Every day, I find countless opportunities to decide whether I will obey God and demonstrate my love for Him or try to please myself or the world system. God is waiting for my choices.

Bill Bright

Christians don't fail to live as they should because they are in the world; they fail because the world has gotten into them.

Billy Graham

To say that a person can come to Christ without making a break from the world is a lie.

John MacArthur

TODAY'S INTEGRITY BUILDER

The world makes plenty of promises that it can't keep. God, on the other hand, keeps every single one of His promises. If you dwell on the world's messages, you're setting yourself up for disaster. If you dwell on God's message, you're setting yourself up for victory.

Pure and undefiled religion before our God and Father is this: to look after orphans and widows in their distress and to keep oneself unstained by the world.

James 1:27 Holman CSB

Now we have not received the spirit of the world, but the Spirit who is from God, in order to know what has been freely given to us by God.

1 Corinthians 2:12 Holman CSB

Do not love the world or the things that belong to the world. If anyone loves the world, love for the Father is not in him.

1 John 2:15 Holman CSB

Do not have other gods besides Me.

Exodus 20:3 Holman CSB

TODAY'S PRAYER

Dear Lord, give me wisdom and perspective. Guide me according to Your plans for my life and according to Your commandments. And keep me mindful, dear Lord, that Your truth is—and will forever be—the ultimate truth. Amen

NEED SOMETHING FROM GOD? ASK!

You do not have because you do not ask.
James 4:2 Holman CSB

How often do you ask God for His help and His wisdom? Occasionally? Intermittently? Whenever you experience a crisis? Hopefully not. Hopefully, you've acquired the habit of asking for God's assistance early and often. And hopefully, you have learned to seek His guidance in every aspect of your life.

Jesus made it clear to His disciples: they should petition God to meet their needs. So should you. Genuine, heartfelt prayer produces powerful changes in you and in your world. When you lift your heart to God, you open yourself to a never-ending source of divine wisdom and infinite love.

James 5:16 makes a promise that God intends to keep: when you pray earnestly, fervently, and often, great things will happen. Too many people, however, are too timid or too pessimistic to ask God to do big things. Please don't count yourself among their number.

God can do great things through you if you have the courage to ask Him (and the determination to keep asking Him). But don't expect Him to do all the work. When you do your part, He will do His part—and when He does, you can expect miracles to happen.

The Bible promises that God will guide you if you let Him. Your job is to let Him. But sometimes, you will be tempted to do otherwise. Sometimes, you'll be tempted to go along with the crowd; other times, you'll be tempted to do things your way, not God's way. When you feel those temptations, resist them.

God has promised that when you ask for His help, He will not withhold it. So ask. Ask Him to meet the needs of your day. Ask Him to lead you, to protect you, and to correct you. Then, trust the answers He gives.

God stands at the door and waits. When you knock, He opens. When you ask, He answers. Your task, of course, is to make God a full partner in every aspect of your life—and to seek His guidance prayerfully, confidently, and often.

We honor God by asking for great things when they are a part of His promise. We dishonor Him and cheat ourselves when we ask for molehills where He has promised mountains.

Vance Havner

We get into trouble when we think we know what to do and we stop asking God if we're doing it.

Stormie Omartian

All we have to do is to acknowledge our need, move from self-sufficiency to dependence, and ask God to become our hiding place.

Bill Hybels

True prayer is measured by weight, not by length. A single groan before God may have more fullness of prayer in it than a fine oration of great length.

C. H. Spurgeon

TODAY'S INTEGRITY BUILDER

Today, think of a specific need that is weighing heavily on your heart. Then, spend a few quiet moments asking God for His guidance and for His help.

What father among you, if his son asks for a fish, will, instead of a fish, give him a snake? Or if he asks for an egg, will give him a scorpion? If you then, who are evil, know how to give good gifts to your children, how much more will the heavenly Father give the Holy Spirit to those who ask Him?

Luke 11:11-13 Holman CSB

So I say to you, keep asking, and it will be given to you. Keep searching, and you will find. Keep knocking, and the door will be opened to you.

Luke 11:9 Holman CSB

Don't worry about anything, but in everything, through prayer and petition with thanksgiving, let your requests be made known to God.

Philippians 4:6 Holman CSB

TODAY'S PRAYER

Lord, today I will ask You for the things I need. In every situation, I will come to You in prayer. You know what I want, Lord, and more importantly, You know what I need. Yet even though I know that You know, I still won't be too timid—or too busy—to ask. Amen

USING THE TALENTS HE GAVE YOU

I remind you to keep ablaze the gift of God that is in you.

2 Timothy 1:6 Holman CSB

All of us have special talents, and you are no exception. But your talent is no guarantee of success; it must be cultivated and nurtured; otherwise, it will go unused . . . and God's gift to you will be squandered.

In the 25th chapter of Matthew, Jesus tells the "Parable of the Talents." In it, He describes a master who leaves his servants with varying amounts of money (talents). When the master returns, some servants have put their money to work and earned more, to which the master responds, "Well done, good and faithful servant! You have been faithful with a few things; I will put you in charge of many things. Come and share your master's happiness!" (Matthew 25:21 NIV)

But the story does not end so happily for the foolish servant who was given a single talent but did nothing with it. For this man, the master has nothing but reproach: "You wicked, lazy servant . . . ." (Matthew 25:26 NIV)

The message from Jesus is clear: We must use our talents, not waste them.

Your particular talent is a treasure on temporary loan from God. He intends that your talent enrich the world and enrich your life. Value the gift that God has given you, nourish it, make it grow, and share it with the world. Then, when you meet your Master face-to-face, you, too, will hear those wonderful words, "Well done, good and faithful servant! . . . Come and share your Master's happiness!"

> You are the only person on earth
> who can use your ability.
>
> —
>
> Zig Ziglar

God often reveals His direction for our lives through the way He made us . . . with a certain personality and unique skills.

Bill Hybels

Employ whatever God has entrusted you with, in doing good, all possible good, in every possible kind and degree.

John Wesley

If you want to reach your potential, you need to add a strong work ethic to your talent.

John Maxwell

What we are is God's gift to us. What we become is our gift to God.

Anonymous

TODAY'S INTEGRITY BUILDER

Converting raw talent into polished skill usually requires work, and lots of it. God's Word clearly instructs you to do the hard work of refining your talents for the glory of His kingdom and the service of His people. So, we are wise to remember the old adage: "What you are is God's gift to you; what you become is your gift to God." And it's up to you to make sure that your gift is worthy of the Giver.

Based on the gift they have received, everyone should use it to serve others, as good managers of the varied grace of God.

1 Peter 4:10 Holman CSB

So he who had received five talents came and brought five other talents, saying, "Lord, you delivered to me five talents; look, I have gained five more talents besides them." His lord said to him, "Well done, good and faithful servant; you were faithful over a few things, I will make you ruler over many things. Enter into the joy of your lord."

Matthew 25:20-21 NKJV

According to the grace given to us, we have different gifts: If prophecy, use it according to the standard of faith; if service, in service; if teaching, in teaching; if exhorting, in exhortation; giving, with generosity; leading, with diligence; showing mercy, with cheerfulness.

Romans 12:6-8 Holman CSB

TODAY'S PRAYER

Father, You have given me abilities to be used for the glory of Your kingdom. Give me the courage and the perseverance to use those talents. Keep me mindful that all my gifts come from You, Lord. Let me be Your faithful, humble servant, and let me give You all the glory and all the praise. Amen

VALUE-BASED DECISIONS

We encouraged, comforted, and implored each one of you
to walk worthy of God,
who calls you into His own kingdom and glory.

1 Thessalonians 2:12 Holman CSB

Whether you realize it or not, your character is shaped by your values. From the time your alarm clock wakes you in the morning until the moment you lay your head on the pillow at night, your actions are guided by the values that you hold most dear. If you're a thoughtful believer, then those values are shaped by the Word of God.

Society seeks to impose its set of values upon you, however these values are often contrary to God's Word (and thus contrary to your own best interests). The world makes promises that it simply cannot fulfill. It promises happiness, contentment, prosperity, and abundance. But genuine abundance is not a byproduct of possessions or status; it is a byproduct of your thoughts, your actions, and your relationship with God. The world's promises are incomplete and deceptive; God's promises are unfailing. Your challenge, then, is to build your value system upon the firm foundation of God's promises . . . nothing else will suffice.

As a citizen of the 21st century, you live in a world that is filled with countless opportunities to make big-time mistakes. The world seems to cry, "Worship me with your time, your money, your energy, and your thoughts!" But God commands otherwise: He commands you to worship Him and Him alone; everything else must be secondary.

Do you want to strengthen your character? If so, then you must build your life upon a value system that puts God first. So, when you're faced with a difficult choice or a powerful temptation, seek God's counsel and trust the counsel that He gives. Invite God into your heart and live according to His commandments. Study His Word and talk to Him often. When you do, you will share in the abundance and peace that only God can give.

Our life pursuits will reflect our character
and personal integrity.

—

Franklin Graham

As the first community to which a person is attached and the first authority under which a person learns to live, the family establishes society's most basic values.

Charles Colson

Sadly, family problems and even financial problems are seldom the real problem, but often the symptom of a weak or nonexistent value system.

Dave Ramsey

Whether you have twenty years left, ten years, one year, one month, one day, or just one hour, there is something very important God wants you to do that can add to His kingdom and your blessing.

Bill Bright

Having values keeps a person focused on the important things.

John Maxwell

TODAY'S INTEGRITY BUILDER

Whose values will you share? You can have the values that the world holds dear, or you can have the values that God holds dear, but you can't have both. The decision is yours . . . and so are the consequences.

Sow righteousness for yourselves and reap faithful love; break up your untilled ground. It is time to seek the Lord until He comes and sends righteousness on you like the rain.

Hosea 10:12 Holman CSB

Teach me, O Lord, the way of Your statutes, and I shall keep it to the end.

Psalm 119:33 NKJV

For it is God who is working among you both the willing and the working for His good purpose.

Philippians 2:13 Holman CSB

Do what is right and good in the Lord's sight, so that you may prosper and so that you may enter and possess the good land the Lord your God swore to [give] your fathers.

Deuteronomy 6:18 Holman CSB

TODAY'S PRAYER

Lord, help me value the things in this world that are really valuable: my life, my family, and my relationship with You. Amen

DAY 58

STRONG ENOUGH TO ENCOURAGE OTHERS

*And let us be concerned about one another
in order to promote love and good works.*

Hebrews 10:24 Holman CSB

Life is a team sport, and all of us need occasional pats on the back from our teammates. This world can be a difficult place, a place where many of our friends and family members are troubled by the challenges of everyday life. And since we cannot always be certain who needs our help, we should strive to speak helpful words to all who cross our paths.

In his letter to the Ephesians, Paul writes, "Do not let any unwholesome talk come out of your mouths, but only what is helpful for building others up according to their needs, that it may benefit those who listen" (v. 29 NIV). This passage reminds us that, as Christians, we are instructed to choose our words carefully so as to build others up through wholesome, honest encouragement. How can we build others up? By celebrating their victories and their accomplishments. As the old saying goes, "When someone does something good, applaud—you'll make two people happy."

Genuine encouragement should never be confused with pity. God intends for His children to lead lives of abundance, joy, celebration and praise—not lives of self-pity or regret. So we must guard ourselves against hosting (or joining) the "pity parties" that so often accompany difficult times. Instead, we must encourage each other to have faith—first in God and His only begotten Son—and then in our own abilities to use the talents God has given us for the furtherance of His kingdom and for the betterment of our own lives.

As a faithful follower of Jesus, you have every reason to be hopeful, and you have every reason to share your hopes with others. When you do, you will discover that hope, like other human emotions, is contagious. So do the world (and yourself) a favor: Look for the good in others and celebrate the good that you find. When you do, you'll be a powerful force of encouragement to your friends and family . . . and a worthy servant to your God.

Do you wonder where you can go for encouragement and motivation? Run to Jesus.

Max Lucado

A lot of people have gone further than they thought they could because someone else thought they could.

Zig Ziglar

In each of my friends there is something that only some other friend can fully bring out. By myself I am not large enough to call the whole man into activity; I want other lights than my own to show all his facets.

C. S. Lewis

Discouraged people don't need critics. They hurt enough already. They don't need more guilt or piled-on distress. They need encouragement. They need a refuge, a willing, caring, available someone.

Charles Swindoll

TODAY'S INTEGRITY BUILDER

Do you want to be successful? Encourage others to do the same. You can't lift other people up without lifting yourself up, too. And remember the words of Oswald Chambers: "God grant that we may not hinder those who are battling their way slowly into the light."

I want their hearts to be encouraged and joined together in love, so that they may have all the riches of assured understanding, and have the knowledge of God's mystery—Christ.

Colossians 2:2 Holman CSB

Carry one another's burdens; in this way you will fulfill the law of Christ.

Galatians 6:2 Holman CSB

But encourage each other daily, while it is still called today, so that none of you is hardened by sin's deception.

Hebrews 3:13 Holman CSB

Anxiety in a man's heart weighs it down, but a good word cheers it up.

Proverbs 12:25 Holman CSB

TODAY'S PRAYER

Dear Lord, make me a man who is quick to celebrate the accomplishments of others. Make me a source of genuine, lasting encouragement to my family and friends. And let my words and deeds be worthy of Your Son, the One who gives me strength and salvation, this day and for all eternity. Amen

BEYOND WORRY

Let not your heart be troubled;
you believe in God, believe also in Me.
John 14:1 NKJV

Because you have the ability to think, you also have the ability to worry. Even if you're a very faithful Christian, you may be plagued by occasional periods of discouragement and doubt. Even though you trust God's promise of salvation—even though you sincerely believe in God's love and protection—you may find yourself upset by the countless details of everyday life. Jesus understood your concerns when He spoke the reassuring words found in the 6th chapter of Matthew.

Therefore I say to you, do not worry about your life, what you will eat or what you will drink; nor about your body, what you will put on. Is not life more than food and the body more than clothing? Look at the birds of the air, for they neither sow nor reap nor gather into barns; yet your heavenly Father feeds them. Are you not of more value than they? Which of you by worrying can add one cubit to his stature? . . . Therefore do not worry about tomorrow, for tomorrow will worry about its own things. Sufficient for the day is its own trouble. (vv. 25-27, 34 NKJV)

Where is the best place to take your worries? Take them to God. Take your troubles to Him; take your fears to Him; take your doubts to Him; take your weaknesses to Him; take your sorrows to Him . . . and leave them all there. Seek protection from the One who offers you eternal salvation; build your spiritual house upon the Rock that cannot be moved.

Perhaps you are concerned about your future, your relationships, or your finances. Or perhaps you are simply a "worrier" by nature. If so, choose to make Matthew 6 a regular part of your daily Bible reading. This beautiful passage will remind you that God still sits in His heaven and you are His beloved child. Then, perhaps, you will worry a little less and trust God a little more, and that's as it should be because God is trustworthy . . . and you are protected.

With the peace of God to guard us and
the God of peace to guide us—why worry?

—

Warren Wiersbe

Much that worries us beforehand can, quite unexpectedly, have a happy and simple solution. Worries just don't matter. Things really are in a better hand than ours.

Dietrich Bonhoeffer

Today is mine. Tomorrow is none of my business. If I peer anxiously into the fog of the future, I will strain my spiritual eyes so that I will not see clearly what is required of me now.

Elisabeth Elliott

The beginning of anxiety is the end of faith, and the beginning of true faith is the end of anxiety.

George Mueller

The more you meditate on God's Word, the less you will have to worry about.

Rick Warren

TODAY'S INTEGRITY BUILDER

Assiduously divide your areas of concern into two categories: those you can control and those you cannot. Resolve never to waste time or energy worrying about the latter.

So don't worry, saying, "What will we eat?" or "What will we drink?" or "What will we wear?" For the Gentiles eagerly seek all these things, and your heavenly Father knows that you need them. But seek first the kingdom of God and His righteousness, and all these things will be provided for you. Therefore don't worry about tomorrow, because tomorrow will worry about itself. Each day has enough trouble of its own.

Matthew 6:31-34 Holman CSB

Come to Me, all you who labor and are heavy laden, and I will give you rest. Take My yoke upon you and learn from Me, for I am gentle and lowly in heart, and you will find rest for your souls. For My yoke is easy and My burden is light.

Matthew 11:28-30 NKJV

Anxiety in a man's heart weighs it down, but a good word cheers it up.

Proverbs 12:25 Holman CSB

TODAY'S PRAYER

Dear Lord, wherever I find myself, let me celebrate more and worry less. When my faith begins to waver, help me to trust You more. Then, with praise on my lips and the love of Your Son in my heart, let me live courageously, faithfully, prayerfully, and thankfully this day and every day. Amen

TOO MANY DISTRACTIONS?

*Let us lay aside every weight and the sin that so easily
ensnares us, and run with endurance
the race that lies before us, keeping our eyes on Jesus,
the source and perfecter of our faith.*

Hebrews 12:1-2 Holman CSB

All of us must live through those days when the traffic jams, the computer crashes, and the dog makes a main course out of our homework. But, when we find ourselves distracted by the minor frustrations of life, we must catch ourselves, take a deep breath, and lift our thoughts upward.

Although we must sometimes struggle mightily to rise above the distractions of the everyday living, we need never struggle alone. God is here—eternal and faithful, with infinite patience and love—and, if we reach out to Him, He will restore our sense of perspective and give peace to our hearts.

Today, as an exercise in character-building, make this promise to yourself and keep it: promise to focus your thoughts on things that are really important, things like your faith, your family, your friends, and your future. Don't allow the day's interruptions to derail your most important work. And don't allow other people (or, for that matter, the media) to decide what's important to you and your family.

Distractions are everywhere, but, thankfully, so is God . . . and that fact has everything to do with how you prioritize your day and your life.

Setting goals is one way you can be sure
that you will focus your efforts on the main things
so that trivial matters will not become your focus.

—

Charles Stanley

When Jesus is in our midst, He brings His limitless power along as well. But, Jesus must be in the middle, all eyes and hearts focused on Him.

Shirley Dobson

This day's bustle and hurly-burly would too often and too soon call us away from Jesus' feet. These distractions must be immediately dismissed, or we shall know only the "barrenness of busyness."

A. W. Tozer

TODAY'S INTEGRITY BUILDER

Take a few minutes to consider the everyday distractions that are interfering with your life and your faith. Then, jot down at least three ideas for minimizing those distractions or eliminating them altogether.

TODAY'S PRAYER

Dear Lord, help me to face this day with a spirit of optimism and thanksgiving. And let me focus my thoughts on You and Your incomparable gifts. Amen

DAY 61

YOUR CHARACTER,
YOUR FAMILY

Choose for yourselves today the one you will worship . . . .
As for me and my family, we will worship the Lord.

Joshua 24:15 Holman CSB

A loving family is a treasure from God. If God has blessed you with a close knit, supportive clan, offer a word of thanks to your Creator because He has given you one of His most precious earthly possessions. Your obligation, in response to God's gift, is to treat your family in ways that are consistent with His commandments.

You live in a fast-paced, demanding world, a place where life can be difficult and pressures can be intense. As those pressures build, you may tend to focus so intently upon your obligations that you lose sight, albeit temporarily, of your spiritual and emotional needs (that's one reason why a regular daily devotional time is so important; it offers a badly-needed dose of perspective).

Even when the demands of everyday life are great, you must never forget that you have been entrusted with a profound responsibility: the responsibility of contributing to your family's emotional and spiritual well-being. It's a big job, but with God's help, you're up to the task.

When you place God squarely in the center of your family's life—when you worship Him, praise Him, trust Him, and love Him—then He will most certainly bless you and yours in ways that you could have scarcely imagined.

So the next time your family life becomes a little stressful, remember this: That little band of men, women, kids, and babies is a priceless treasure on temporary loan from the Father above. And it's your responsibility to praise God for that gift—and to act accordingly.

You have heard about "quality time" and
"quantity time." Your family needs both.

—

Jim Gallery

When you think about it for a moment, it certainly makes sense that if people can establish a loving and compatible relationship at home, they have a better chance of establishing winning relationships with those with whom they work on a regular basis.

Zig Ziglar

More than any other single factor in a person's formative years, family life forges character.

John Maxwell

The only true source of meaning in life is found in love for God and his son Jesus Christ, and love for mankind, beginning with our own families.

James Dobson

Never give your family the leftovers and crumbs of your time.

Charles Swindoll

TODAY'S INTEGRITY BUILDER

Today, think about the importance of saying "yes" to your family even if it means saying "no" to other obligations.

Love must be without hypocrisy. Detest evil; cling to what is good. Show family affection to one another with brotherly love. Outdo one another in showing honor.

Romans 12:9–10 Holman CSB

If a kingdom is divided against itself, that kingdom cannot stand. If a house is divided against itself, that house cannot stand.

Mark 3:24-25 Holman CSB

Now if anyone does not provide for his own relatives, and especially for his household, he has denied the faith and is worse than an unbeliever.

1 Timothy 5:8 Holman CSB

Let them first learn to show piety at home and to repay their parents; for this is good and acceptable before God.

1 Timothy 5:4 NKJV

TODAY'S PRAYER

Dear Lord, I am part of Your family, and I praise You for Your gifts and Your love. Father, You have also blessed me with my earthly family. Let me show love and acceptance for my own family so that through me, they might come to know You. Amen

DAY 62

REBELLION INVITES DISASTER

You must follow the Lord your God and fear Him.
You must keep His commands and listen to His voice;
you must worship Him and remain faithful to Him.

Deuteronomy 13:4 Holman CSB

For most of us, it is a daunting thought: one day, perhaps soon, we'll come face to face with our Heavenly Father, and we'll be called to account for our actions here on earth. Our personal histories will certainly not be surprising to God; He already knows everything about us. But the full scope of our activities may be surprising to us: some of us will be pleasantly surprised; others will not be.

God's commandments are not offered as helpful hints or timely tips. God's commandments are not suggestions; they are ironclad rules for living, rules that we disobey at our own risk.

The English clergyman Thomas Fuller observed, "He does not believe who does not live according to his beliefs." These words are most certainly true. We may proclaim our beliefs to our hearts' content, but our proclamations will mean nothing—to others or to ourselves—unless we accompany our words with deeds that match. The sermons that we live are far more compelling than the ones we preach.

So today, do whatever you can to ensure that your thoughts and your deeds are pleasing to your Creator. Because you will, at some point in the future, be called to account for your actions. And the future may be sooner than you think.

Sin is largely a matter of mistaken priorities.
Any sin in us that is cherished, hidden,
and not confessed will cut the nerve center of our faith.

—

Catherine Marshall

The Fall is simply and solely Disobedience—doing what you have been told not to do: and it results from Pride—from being too big for your boots, forgetting your place, thinking that you are God.

C. S. Lewis

Let us never suppose that obedience is impossible or that holiness is meant only for a select few. Our Shepherd leads us in paths of righteousness—not for our name's sake but for His.

Elisabeth Elliot

Only he who believes is obedient, and only he who is obedient believes.

Dietrich Bonhoeffer

As I have continued to grow in my Christian maturity, I have discovered that the Holy Spirit does not let me get by with anything.

Anne Graham Lotz

TODAY'S INTEGRITY BUILDER

Be honest with yourself as you consider ways that you have, in the last few days, disobeyed God. Then, think about specific ways that you can be more obedient today.

237

And the world with its lust is passing away, but the one who does God's will remains forever.

1 John 2:17 Holman CSB

Therefore, get your minds ready for action, being self-disciplined, and set your hope completely on the grace to be brought to you at the revelation of Jesus Christ. As obedient children, do not be conformed to the desires of your former ignorance but, as the One who called you is holy, you also are to be holy in all your conduct.

1 Peter 1:13-15 Holman CSB

But Peter and the apostles replied, "We must obey God rather than men."

Acts 5:29 Holman CSB

TODAY'S PRAYER

Heavenly Father, when I turn my thoughts away from You and Your Word, I suffer. But when I obey Your commandments, when I place my faith in You, I am secure. Let me live according to Your commandments. Direct my path far from the temptations and distractions of this world. And, let me discover Your will and follow it, Dear Lord, this day and always. Amen

HUMILITY STRENGTHENS CHARACTER

Therefore, God's chosen ones, holy and loved,
put on heartfelt compassion, kindness,
humility, gentleness, and patience.
Colossians 3:12 Holman CSB

We have heard the phrases on countless occasions: "He's a self-made man." In truth, none of us are self-made. We all owe countless debts that we can never repay.

Our first debt, of course, is to our Father in heaven—who has given us everything—and to His Son who sacrificed His own life so that we might live eternally. We are also indebted to ancestors, parents, teachers, friends, spouses, family members, coworkers, fellow believers . . . and the list, of course, goes on.

As Christians, we have a profound reason to be humble: We have been refashioned and saved by Jesus Christ, and that salvation came not because of our own good works but because of God's grace. Thus, we are not "self-made"; we are "God-made" and "Christ-saved." How, then, can we be boastful? The answer, of course, is that, if we are honest with ourselves and with our God, we simply can't be boastful . . . we must, instead, be eternally grateful and exceedingly humble.

Humility is not, in most cases, a naturally-occurring human trait. Most of us, it seems, are more than willing to stick out our chests and say, "Look at me; I did that!" But in our better moments, in the quiet moments when we search the depths of our own hearts, we know better. Whatever "it" is, God did that, not us.

St. Augustine observed, "If you plan to build a tall house of virtues, you must first lay deep foundations of humility." Are you a believer who genuinely seeks to build your house of virtues on a strong foundation of humility? If so, you are wise and you are blessed. But if you've been laboring under the misconception that you're a "self-made" man, it's time to strengthen your character by facing this simple fact: your blessings come from God. And He deserves the credit.

Jesus had a humble heart. If He abides in us, pride will never dominate our lives.

Billy Graham

It was pride that changed angels into devils; it is humility that makes men as angels.

St. Augustine

Humility is not thinking less of yourself; it is thinking of yourself less.

Rick Warren

The great characteristic of the saint is humility.

Oswald Chambers

Humility is a thing which must be genuine; the imitation of it is the nearest thing in the world to pride.

C. H. Spurgeon

Today's Integrity Builder

Remember that humility leads to happiness, and pride doesn't. Max Lucado writes, "God exalts humility. When God works in our lives, helping us to become humble, he gives us a permanent joy. Humility gives us a joy that cannot be taken away." Enough said.

Clothe yourselves with humility toward one another, because God resists the proud, but gives grace to the humble.

1 Peter 5:5 Holman CSB

Humble yourselves therefore under the mighty hand of God, so that He may exalt you in due time, casting all your care upon Him, because He cares about you.

1 Peter 5:6-7 Holman CSB

But He said to me, "My grace is sufficient for you, for power is perfected in weakness." Therefore, I will most gladly boast all the more about my weaknesses, so that Christ's power may reside in me.

2 Corinthians 12:9 Holman CSB

TODAY'S PRAYER

Heavenly Father, Jesus clothed Himself with humility when He chose to leave heaven and come to earth to live and die for us, His children. Christ is my Master and my example. Clothe me with humility, Lord, so that I might be more like Your Son, and keep me mindful that You are the giver and sustainer of life, and to You, Dear Lord, goes the glory and the praise. Amen

EMBRACING GOD'S LOVE

The one who trusts in the Lord will have
faithful love surrounding him.
Psalm 32:10 Holman CSB

Have you formed the character-building habit of accepting and sharing God's love? Hopefully so. After all, God's love for you is bigger and better than you can imagine. In fact, God's love is far too big to comprehend (in this lifetime). But this much we do know: God loves you so much that He sent His Son Jesus to come to this earth and to die for you. And, when you accepted Jesus into your heart, God gave you a gift that is more precious than gold: the gift of eternal life. Now, precisely because you are a wondrous creation treasured by God, a question presents itself: What will you do in response to God's love? Will you ignore it or embrace it? Will you return it or neglect it? Will you receive it and share it . . . or not? The answer to these simple questions will determine the level of your faith and the quality of your life.

When you form the habit of embracing God's love day in and day out, you feel differently about yourself, your neighbors, and your world. When you embrace God's love, you share His message and you obey His commandments.

When you accept the Father's gift of grace, you are blessed here on earth and throughout all eternity. So do yourself a favor right now: accept God's love with open arms and welcome His Son Jesus into your heart.

Corrie ten Boom observed, "We must mirror God's love in the midst of a world full of hatred. We are the mirrors of God's love, so we may show Jesus by our lives." And her words most certainly apply to Christian family, including yours.

God's heart is overflowing with love for you and yours. Accept that love. Return that love. Respect that love. And share that love. Today.

If you have an obedience problem,
you have a love problem.
Focus your attention on God's love.

—

Henry Blackaby

Even when we cannot see the why and wherefore of God's dealings, we know that there is love in and behind them, so we can rejoice always.

J. I. Packer

The love of God is one of the great realities of the universe, a pillar upon which the hope of the world rests. But it is a personal, intimate thing too. God does not love populations. He loves people. He loves not masses, but men.

A. W. Tozer

The life of faith is a daily exploration of the constant and countless ways in which God's grace and love are experienced.

Eugene Peterson

TODAY'S INTEGRITY BUILDER

God's love is our greatest security blanket. Kay Arthur advises, "Snuggle in God's arms. When you are hurting, when you feel lonely or left out, let Him cradle you, comfort you, reassure you of His all-sufficient power and love." Enough said.

God is love, and the one who remains in love remains in God, and God remains in him.

1 John 4:16 Holman CSB

As the Father loved Me, I also have loved you; abide in My love.

John 15:9 NKJV

For God so loved the world, that he gave his only begotten Son, that whosoever believeth in him should not perish, but have everlasting life.

John 3:16 KJV

[Because of] the Lord's faithful love we do not perish, for His mercies never end.

Lamentations 3:22 Holman CSB

TODAY'S PRAYER

Thank You, Dear God, for Your love. You are my loving Father. I thank You for Your love and for Your Son. I will praise You; I will worship You; and, I will love You today, tomorrow, and forever. Amen

WITH WISDOM COMES CHARACTER

Who is wise and understanding among you?
He should show his works by good conduct
with wisdom's gentleness.

James 3:13 Holman CSB

D o you place a high value on the acquisition of wisdom? If so, you are not alone; most people would like to be wise, but not everyone is willing to do the work that is required to become wise. Wisdom is not like a mushroom; it does not spring up overnight. It is, instead, like an oak tree that starts as a tiny acorn, grows into a sapling, and eventually reaches up to the sky, tall and strong.

To become wise, you must seek God's guidance and live according to His Word. To become wise, you must seek instruction with consistency and purpose. To become wise, you must not only learn the lessons of the Christian life, but you must also live by them. But oftentimes, that's easier said than done.

Sometimes, amid the demands of daily life, you will lose perspective. Life may seem out of balance, and the pressures of everyday living may seem overwhelming. What's needed is a fresh perspective, a restored sense of balance . . . and God's wisdom. If you call upon the Lord and seek to see the world through His eyes, He will give you guidance, wisdom, and perspective. When you make God's priorities your priorities, He will lead you according to His plan and according to His commandments. When you study God's teachings, you are reminded that God's reality is the ultimate reality.

Do you seek to live a life of righteousness and wisdom? If so, you must study the ultimate source of wisdom: the Word of God. You must seek out worthy mentors and listen carefully to their advice. You must associate, day in and day out, with godly men and women. Then, as you accumulate wisdom, you must not keep it for yourself; you must, instead, share it with your friends and family members.

But be forewarned: if you sincerely seek to share your hard-earned wisdom with others, your actions must reflect the values that you hold dear. The best way to share your wisdom—perhaps the only way—is not by your words, but by your example.

The more wisdom enters our hearts, the more we will be able to trust our hearts in difficult situations.

John Eldredge

No matter how many books you read, no matter how many schools you attend, you're never really wise until you start making wise choices.

Marie T. Freeman

The essence of wisdom, from a practical standpoint, is pausing long enough to look at our lives—invitations, opportunities, relationships—from God's perspective. And then acting on it.

Charles Stanley

If you lack knowledge, go to school. If you lack wisdom, get on your knees.

Vance Havner

TODAY'S INTEGRITY BUILDER

Need wisdom? God's got it. If you want it, then study God's Word and associate with godly people.

The fear of the Lord is the beginning of wisdom; a good understanding have all those who do His commandments. His praise endures forever.

Psalm 111:10 NKJV

Therefore, everyone who hears these words of Mine and acts on them will be like a sensible man who built his house on the rock. The rain fell, the rivers rose, and the winds blew and pounded that house. Yet it didn't collapse, because its foundation was on the rock.

Matthew 7:24–25 Holman CSB

A wise man will hear and increase learning, and a man of understanding will attain wise counsel.

Proverbs 1:5 NKJV

Teach me, O Lord, the way of Your statutes, and I shall keep it to the end.

Psalm 119:33 NKJV

TODAY'S PRAYER

Lord, make me a man of wisdom and discernment. I seek wisdom, Lord, not from this world, but from You. Lead me in Your ways and teach me from Your Word so that, in time, my wisdom might glorify Your kingdom and Your Son. Amen

ASSERTING YOURSELF AND PROTECTING YOUR INTEGRITY

For God has not given us a spirit of fearfulness,
but one of power, love, and sound judgment.

2 Timothy 1:7 Holman CSB

When Paul wrote Timothy, he reminded his young protégé that the God he served was a bold God and that God's spirit empowered His children with boldness also. Like Timothy, we, too, face times of uncertainty and fear in the ever-changing world in which we live. God's message is the same to us today as it was to Timothy: We can live boldly because the spirit of God resides in us.

When your friends encourage you to do things that you know are wrong, are you bold enough to say no? Hopefully so. But if you haven't quite learned the fine art of assertiveness, don't feel like the Lone Ranger—plenty of people, even grown men who are old enough to know better, still have trouble standing up for themselves.

If you really want to strengthen your character, you have no alternative—you must be assertive. Why? Because assertiveness is an essential component of a strong character. With assertiveness, you can stand on your own two feet; without it, you are doomed to follow the crowd wherever they may choose to go (and oftentimes, they choose to go in the wrong direction).

You're almost never too old to learn how to become more assertive. So do yourself this major league favor: learn to say no politely, firmly, and often. When you do, you'll be protecting yourself and your character.

We are never stronger than the moment
we admit we are weak.

—

Beth Moore

God would rather have a man on the wrong side of the fence than on the fence. The worst enemies of apostles are not the opposers but the appeasers.

Vance Havner

Chiefly the mold of a man's fortune is in his own hands.

Francis Bacon

Jesus Christ's teaching never beats about the bush.

Oswald Chambers

The strength that we claim from God's Word does not depend on circumstances. Circumstances will be difficult, but our strength will be sufficient.

Corrie ten Boom

TODAY'S INTEGRITY BUILDER

Today, ask yourself if you're being assertive enough at work, at home, or in between. If the answer is no, decide on at three specific steps you can take to stand up for yourself appropriately, fairly, and often.

Therefore, we may boldly say: The Lord is my helper; I will not be afraid. What can man do to me?

Hebrews 13:6 Holman CSB

The one who acquires good sense loves himself; one who safeguards understanding finds success.

Proverbs 19:8 Holman CSB

For it was You who created my inward parts; You knit me together in my mother's womb. I will praise You, because I have been remarkably and wonderfully made.

Psalm 139:13-14 Holman CSB

For by the grace given to me, I tell everyone among you not to think of himself more highly than he should think. Instead, think sensibly, as God has distributed a measure of faith to each one.

Romans 12:3 Holman CSB

TODAY'S PRAYER

Lord, I have so much to learn and so many ways to improve myself, but You love me just as I am. Thank You for Your love and for Your Son. And, help me to become the person that You want me to become. Amen

CHRIST-CENTERED LEADERSHIP

Those who are wise will shine like the bright expanse
[of the heavens], and those who lead many to righteousness,
like the stars forever and ever.

Daniel 12:3 Holman CSB

The old saying is familiar and true: imitation is the sincerest form of flattery. As believers, we are called to imitate, as best we can, the carpenter from Galilee. The task of imitating Christ is often difficult and sometimes impossible, but as Christians, we must continue to try.

Our world needs leaders who willingly honor Christ with their words and their deeds, but not necessarily in that order. If you seek to be such a leader, then you must begin by making yourself a worthy example to your family, to your friends, to your church, and to your community. After all, your words of instruction will never ring true unless you yourself are willing to follow them.

Christ-centered leadership is an exercise in service: service to God in heaven and service to His children here on earth. Christ willingly became a servant to His follow-ers, and you must seek to do the same for yours.

Are you the kind of servant-leader whom you would want to follow? If so, congratulations: You are honoring your Savior by imitating Him. And that, of course, is the sincerest form of flattery.

Leadership is found in becoming the servant of all.

—

Richard Foster

True leaders are not afraid to surround themselves with people of ability—and not afraid to give those people opportunities for greatness.

Warren Wiersbe

The goal of leadership is to empower the whole people of God to discern and to discharge the Lord's will.

Stanley Grenz

The test of a leader is taking the vision from me to we.

John Maxwell

A true and safe leader is likely to be one who has no desire to lead, but is forced into a position of leadership by inward pressure of the Holy Spirit and the press of external situation.

A. W. Tozer

TODAY'S INTEGRITY BUILDER

In thinking about your leadership style, ask yourself this: who's your model? If you're wise, you'll try, as best you can, to emulate Jesus.

Shepherd God's flock among you, not overseeing out of compulsion but freely, according to God's will; not for the money but eagerly.

1 Peter 5:2 Holman CSB

An overseer, therefore, must be above reproach, the husband of one wife, self-controlled, sensible, respectable, hospitable, an able teacher, not addicted to wine, not a bully but gentle, not quarrelsome, not greedy.

1 Timothy 3:2-3 Holman CSB

Those who are wise will shine like the bright expanse [of the heavens], and those who lead many to righteousness, like the stars forever and ever.

Daniel 12:3 Holman CSB

TODAY'S PRAYER

Heavenly Father, when I find myself in a position of leadership, let me follow Your teachings and obey Your commandments. Make me a person of integrity and wisdom, Lord, and make me a worthy example to those whom I serve. And, let me turn to You, Lord, for guidance and for strength in all that I say and do. Amen

KEEPING A PROPER
PERSPECTIVE

All I'm doing right now, friends, is showing how these things
pertain to Apollos and me so that you will learn restraint and
not rush into making judgments without knowing all the facts.
It is important to look at things from God's point of view.
I would rather not see you inflating or
deflating reputations based on mere hearsay.

1 Corinthians 4:6 MSG

For most of us, life is busy and complicated. Amid the rush and crush of the daily grind, it is easy to lose perspective . . . easy, but wrong. When the world seems to be spinning out of control, we can regain perspective by slowing ourselves down and then turning our thoughts and prayers toward God.

The familiar words of Psalm 46:10 remind us to "Be still, and know that I am God" (NKJV). When we do so, we are reminded of God's love (not to mention God's priorities), and we can then refocus our thoughts on the things that matter most. But, when we ignore the presence of our Creator—if we rush from place to place with scarcely a spare minute for God—we rob ourselves of His perspective, His peace, and His joy.

Do you carve out quiet moments each day to offer thanksgiving and praise to your Creator? You should. During these moments of stillness, you will often sense the love and wisdom of our Lord.

Today and every day, make time to be still before God. When you do, you can face the day's complications with the wisdom, the perspective, and the power that only He can provide.

Joy is the direct result of having God's perspective on our daily lives and the effect of loving our Lord enough to obey His commands and trust His promises.

—

Bill Bright

What you see and hear depends a good deal on where you are standing; it also depends on what sort of person you are.

C. S. Lewis

When you and I hurt deeply, what we really need is not an explanation from God but a revelation of God. We need to see how great God is; we need to recover our lost perspective on life. Things get out of proportion when we are suffering, and it takes a vision of something bigger than ourselves to get life's dimensions adjusted again.

Warren Wiersbe

Earthly fears are no fears at all. Answer the big question of eternity, and the little questions of life fall into perspective.

Max Lucado

TODAY'S INTEGRITY BUILDER

Keep life in perspective. Remember that your life is an integral part of God's grand plan. So don't become unduly upset over the minor inconveniences of life, and don't worry too much about today's setbacks—they're temporary.

Now if any of you lacks wisdom, he should ask God, who gives to all generously and without criticizing, and it will be given to him.

James 1:5 Holman CSB

For now we see in a mirror, dimly, but then face to face. Now I know in part, but then I shall know just as I also am known.

1 Corinthians 13:12 NKJV

Let no one deceive himself. If anyone among you seems to be wise in this age, let him become a fool that he may become wise. For the wisdom of this world is foolishness with God. For it is written, "He catches the wise in their own craftiness."

1 Corinthians 3:18-19 NKJV

Acquire wisdom—how much better it is than gold! And acquire understanding—it is preferable to silver.

Proverbs 16:16 Holman CSB

TODAY'S PRAYER

Dear Lord, when the pace of my life becomes frantic, slow me down and give me perspective. Give me the wisdom to realize that the problems of today are only temporary but that Your love is eternal. When I become discouraged, keep me steady and sure, so that I might do Your will here on earth and then live with You forever in heaven. Amen

GETTING TO KNOW GOD BUILDS CHARACTER

*For this very reason, make every effort to supplement
your faith with goodness, goodness with knowledge,
knowledge with self-control, self-control with endurance,
endurance with godliness.*

2 Peter 1:5-6 Holman CSB

If you'd like to strengthen your character, try spending more time really getting to know God. How can you do it? Through worship, praise, Bible study, prayer, and silent meditation.

Do you ever wonder if God is really "right here, right now"? Do you wonder if God hears your prayers, if He understands your feelings, or if He really knows your heart? When you have doubts about your Father in heaven, remember this: God isn't on a coffee break, and He hasn't moved out of town. He's right here, right now, listening to your thoughts and prayers, watching over your every move.

The Bible teaches that a wonderful way to get to know God is simply to be still and listen to Him. But sometimes, you may find it hard to slow yourself down long enough to quiet your mind and tune up your heart. And as the demands of everyday life weigh down upon you, you may be tempted to ignore God's presence or—worse yet—to rebel against His commandments. But, when you quiet yourself and acknowledge His presence, God touches your heart and restores your spirits. So why not let Him do it right now? If you really want to know Him better, silence is a wonderful place to start.

We can seek God and find him!
God is knowable, touchable, hearable, seeable,
with the mind, the hands,
the ears, and eyes of the inner man.
A. W. Tozer

You cannot grow spiritually until you have the assurance that Christ is in your life.

Vonette Bright

God wants to be in an intimate relationship with you. He's the God who has orchestrated every event of your life to give you the best chance to get to know Him, so that you can experience the full measure of His love.

Bill Hybels

Christians have spent their whole lives mastering all sorts of principles, done their duty, carried on the programs of their church . . . and never known God intimately, heart to heart.

John Eldredge

Here is our opportunity: we cannot see God, but we can see Christ. Christ was not only the Son of God, but He was the Father. Whatever Christ was, that God is.

Hannah Whitall Smith

TODAY'S INTEGRITY BUILDER

If you'd like to get to know God a little better, talk to Him more often. The more often you speak to Him, the more often He'll speak to you.

Be still, and know that I am God.

Psalm 46:10 NKJV

You shall have no other gods before Me.

Exodus 20:3 NKJV

For it is written, "You shall worship the Lord your God, and Him only you shall serve."

Matthew 4:10 NKJV

The one who does not love does not know God, because God is love.

1 John 4:8 Holman CSB

TODAY'S PRAYER

Dear Lord, help me remember the importance of silence. Help me discover quiet moments throughout the day so that I can sense Your presence and Your love. Amen

DAY 70

SUBTLE IMMORALITY

*For everyone who practices wicked things hates the light
and avoids it, so that his deeds may not be exposed.
But anyone who lives by the truth comes to the light,
so that his works may be shown to be accomplished by God.*
John 3:20–21 Holman CSB

Sometimes sin has a way of sneaking up on us. In the beginning, we don't intend to rebel against God—in fact, we don't think much about God at all. We think, instead, about the allure of sin, and we think (quite incorrectly) that sin is "harmless."

If we deny our sins, we allow those sins to flourish. And if we allow sinful behaviors to become habits, we invite certain hardships into our own lives and into the lives of our loved ones.

Sin tears down character. When we yield to the distractions and temptations of this troubled world, we suffer. But God has other intentions, and His plans for our lives do not include sin or denial.

As creatures of free will, we may disobey God whenever we choose, but when we do so, we put ourselves and our loved ones in peril. Why? Because disobedience invites disaster. We cannot sin against God without consequence. We cannot live outside His will without injury. We cannot distance ourselves from God without hardening our hearts. We cannot yield to the ever-tempting distractions of our world and, at the same time, enjoy God's peace.

Sometimes, in a futile attempt to justify our behaviors, we make a distinction between "big" sins and "little" ones. To do so is a mistake of "big" proportions. Sins of all shapes and sizes have the power to do us great harm. And in a world where sin is big business, that's certainly a sobering thought.

The power of the resurrection of Jesus Christ
is a power that could overcome every spiritual failing,
every sin, every weakness, in one explosive act.

—

Bill Hybels

What I like about experience is that it is such an honest thing. You may take any number of wrong turnings; but keep your eyes open and you will not be allowed to go very far before the warning signs appear. You may have deceived yourself, but experience is not trying to deceive you. The universe rings true wherever you fairly test it.

C. S. Lewis

Abide in Jesus, the sinless one—which means, give up all of self and its life, and dwell in God's will and rest in His strength. This is what brings the power that does not commit sin.

Andrew Murray

Don't be bound by your guilt or your fears any longer, but realize that sin's penalty has already been paid by Christ completely and fully.

Billy Graham

TODAY'S INTEGRITY BUILDER

Sometimes immorality is obvious and sometimes it's not. So beware: the most subtle forms of sin are the most dangerous.

If we say that we have no sin, we deceive ourselves, and the truth is not in us. If we confess our sins, He is faithful and just to forgive us our sins and to cleanse us from all unrighteousness.

1 John 1:8-9 NKJV

Whoever transgresses and does not abide in the doctrine of Christ does not have God. He who abides in the doctrine of Christ has both the Father and the Son.

2 John 1:9 NKJV

Let us lay aside every weight, and the sin which so easily ensnares us, and let us run with endurance the race that is set before us.

Hebrews 12:1 NKJV

TODAY'S PRAYER

Dear Lord, when I displease You, I do injury to myself, to my family, and to my community. Because sin distances me from You, Lord, I will fear sin and I will avoid sinful places. The fear of sinning against You is a healthy fear, Father, because it can motivate me to accomplish Your will. Let a healthy fear of sin guide my path, today and every day of my life. Amen

HE IS SUFFICIENT

And He said to me, "My grace is sufficient for you,
for My strength is made perfect in weakness."
2 Corinthians 12:9 NKJV

Of this you can be certain: God is sufficient to meet your needs. Period.

Do the demands of life seem overwhelming at times? If so, you must learn to rely not only upon your own resources, but also upon the promises of your Father in heaven. God will hold your hand and walk with you and your family if you let Him. So even if your circumstances are difficult, trust the Father.

The Psalmist writes, "Weeping may endure for a night, but joy comes in the morning" (Psalm 30:5 NKJV). But when we are suffering, the morning may seem very far away. It is not. God promises that He is "near to those who have a broken heart" (Psalm 34:18 NKJV). When we are troubled, we must turn to Him, and we must encourage our friends and family members to do likewise.

If you are discouraged by the inevitable demands of life here on earth, be mindful of this fact: the loving heart of God is sufficient to meet any challenge . . . including yours.

Jesus has been consistently affectionate and true to us. He has shared his great wealth with us. How can we doubt the all-powerful, all-sufficient Lord?

C. H. Spurgeon

God's saints in all ages have realized that God was enough for them. God is enough for time; God is enough for eternity. God is enough!

Hannah Whitall Smith

Yes, God's grace is always sufficient, and His arms are always open to give it. But, will our arms be open to receive it?

Beth Moore

The promises of God's Word sustain us in our suffering, and we know Jesus sympathizes and empathizes with us in our darkest hour.

Bill Bright

TODAY'S INTEGRITY BUILDER

If you'd like infinite protection, there's only one place you can receive it: from an infinite God. So remember: when you live in the center of God's will, you will also be living in the center of God's protection.

Now the God of all grace, who called you to His eternal glory in Christ Jesus, will personally restore, establish, strengthen, and support you.

1 Peter 5:10 Holman CSB

Peace, peace to you, and peace to your helpers! For your God helps you.

1 Chronicles 12:18 NKJV

The LORD is my strength and song, and He has become my salvation; He is my God, and I will praise Him . . .

Exodus 15:2 NKJV

Therefore whoever hears these sayings of Mine, and does them, I will liken him to a wise man who built his house on the rock: and the rain descended, the floods came, and the winds blew and beat on that house; and it did not fall, for it was founded on the rock.

Matthew 7:24-25 NKJV

TODAY'S PRAYER

Dear Lord, as I face the challenges of this day, You protect me. I thank You, Father, for Your love and for Your strength. I will lean upon You today and forever. Amen

FAMILY
FRIENDS
JOB
RIGHT CHOICES

CONTROLLING YOUR TEMPER

Everyone must be quick to hear, slow to speak,
and slow to anger, for man's anger
does not accomplish God's righteousness.
James 1:19-20 Holman CSB

The frustrations of everyday living can sometimes get the better of us, and we allow minor disappointments to cause us major problems. When we allow ourselves to become overly irritated by the inevitable ups and downs of life, we may become overstressed, overheated, overanxious, and just plain angry.

Anger often leads to impulsivity; impulsivity often leads to poor decision-making; and poor decision-making tends to tear down character. So, if you'd like to increase your storehouse of wisdom while, at the same time, strengthening your character, you should learn to control your temper before your temper controls you.

When you allow yourself to become angry, you are certain to defeat at least one person: yourself. When you allow the minor frustrations of everyday life to hijack your emotions, you do harm to yourself and to your loved ones. So today and every day, guard yourself against the kind of angry thinking that inevitably takes a toll on your emotions and your relationships.

As the old saying goes, "Anger usually improves nothing but the arch of a cat's back." So don't allow feelings of anger or frustration to rule your life, or, for that matter, your day—your life is simply too short for that, and you deserve much better treatment than that . . . from yourself.

Anger breeds remorse in the heart,
discord in the home, bitterness in the community,
and confusion in the state.

—

Billy Graham

Anger is the noise of the soul; the unseen irritant of the heart; the relentless invader of silence.

Max Lucado

Bitterness and anger, usually over trivial things, make havoc of homes, churches, and friendships.

Warren Wiersbe

When you strike out in anger, you may miss the other person, but you will always hit yourself.

Jim Gallery

Anger is the fluid that love bleeds when you cut it.

C. S. Lewis

Anger's the anaesthetic of the mind.

C. S. Lewis

TODAY'S INTEGRITY BUILDER

If you think you're about to explode in anger, don't! Instead of striking back at someone, it's usually better to slow down, catch your breath, consider your options, and walk away if you must. Striking out in anger can lead to big problems. So it's better to walk away—and keep walking—than to blurt out angry words that can't be un-blurted.

Don't neglect to show hospitality, for by doing this some have welcomed angels as guests without knowing it.

Hebrews 13:2 Holman CSB

For He will give His angels orders concerning you, to protect you in all your ways.

Psalm 91:11 Holman CSB

The harvest is the end of the age, and the harvesters are angels.

Matthew 13:39 Holman CSB

For the Son of Man is going to come with His angels in the glory of His Father, and then He will reward each according to what he has done.

Matthew 16:27 Holman CSB

TODAY'S PRAYER

Lord, when I become angry, help me to remember that You offer me peace. Let me turn to You for wisdom, for patience, and for the peace that only You can give. Amen

MAKING PEACE WITH THE PAST

Do not remember the past events, pay no attention to things
of old. Look, I am about to do something new;
even now it is coming. Do you not see it? Indeed,
I will make a way in the wilderness, rivers in the desert.
Isaiah 43:18-19 Holman CSB

The American theologian Reinhold Niebuhr composed a profoundly simple verse that came to be known as the Serenity Prayer: "God, grant me the serenity to accept the things I cannot change, the courage to change the things I can, and the wisdom to know the difference." Niebuhr's words are far easier to recite than they are to live by. Why? Because most of us want life to unfold in accordance with our own wishes and timetables. But sometimes God has other plans.

One of the things that fits nicely into the category of "things we cannot change" is the past. Yet even though we know that the past is unchangeable, many of us continue to invest energy worrying about the unfairness of yesterday (when we should, instead, be focusing on the opportunities of today and the promises of tomorrow). Author Hannah Whitall Smith observed, "How changed our lives would be if we could only fly through the days on wings of surrender and trust!" These words remind us that even when we cannot understand the past, we must trust God and accept His will.

So, if you've endured a difficult past, accept it and learn from it, but don't spend too much time here in the precious present fretting over memories of the unchange-able past. Instead, trust God's plan and look to the future. After all, the future is where everything that's going to happen to you from this moment on is going to take place.

You cannot restore your relationship with God,
and I cannot restore mine. We cannot change
the past . . . . God has done what you and I could not:
sent His Son to be the peace offering He requires.

—

Ed Young

Shake the dust from your past, and move forward in His promises.

Kay Arthur

Don't let yesterday use up too much of today.

Dennis Swanberg

Our yesterdays present irreparable things to us; it is true that we have lost opportunities which will never return, but God can transform this destructive anxiety into a constructive thoughtfulness for the future. Let the past sleep, but let it sleep on the bosom of Christ. Leave the Irreparable Past in His hands, and step out into the Irresistible Future with Him.

Oswald Chambers

The devil keeps so many of us stuck in our weakness. He reminds us of our pasts when we ought to remind him of his future—he doesn't have one.

Franklin Graham

TODAY'S INTEGRITY BUILDER

The past is past, so don't live there. If you're focused on the past, change your focus. If you're living in the past, it's time to stop living there, starting now.

All bitterness, anger and wrath, insult and slander must be removed from you, along with all wickedness. And be kind and compassionate to one another, forgiving one another, just as God also forgave you in Christ.

Ephesians 4:31-32 Holman CSB

Should we accept only good from God and not adversity?

Job 2:10 Holman CSB

I have learned, in whatsoever state I am, therewith to be content.

Philippians 4:11 KJV

Brothers, I do not consider myself to have taken hold of it. But one thing I do: forgetting what is behind and reaching forward to what is ahead, I pursue as my goal the prize promised by God's heavenly call in Christ Jesus.

Philippians 3:13-14 Holman CSB

TODAY'S PRAYER

Heavenly Father, free me from anger, resentment, and envy. When I am bitter, I cannot feel the peace that You intend for my life. Keep me mindful that forgiveness is Your commandment, and help me accept the past, treasure the present, and trust the future . . . to You. Amen

DAY 74

PROBLEM-SOLVING BUILDS CHARACTER

*Many adversities come to the one who is righteous,
but the Lord delivers him from them all.*

Psalm 34:19 Holman CSB

Life is an adventure in problem-solving. The question is not whether we will encounter problems; the real question is how we will choose to address them. When it comes to solving the problems of everyday living, we often know precisely what needs to be done, but we may be slow in doing it—especially if what needs to be done is difficult. So we put off till tomorrow what should be done today.

As a person living here in the 21st century, you have your own set of challenges. As you face those challenges, you may be comforted by this fact: Trouble, of every kind, is temporary. Yet God's grace is eternal. And worries, of every kind, are temporary. But God's love is everlasting. The troubles that concern you will pass. God remains. And for every problem, God has a solution.

The words of Psalm 34 remind us that the Lord solves problems for "people who do what is right." And usually, doing "what is right" means doing the uncomfortable work of confronting our problems sooner rather than later. So with no further ado, let the problem-solving begin . . . right now.

Life will be made or broken at the place
where we meet and deal with obstacles.

—

E. Stanley Jones

We are all faced with a series of great opportunities, brilliantly disguised as unsolvable problems. Unsolvable without God's wisdom, that is.

Charles Swindoll

Each problem is a God-appointed instructor.

Charles Swindoll

God is bigger than your problems. Whatever worries press upon you today, put them in God's hands and leave them there.

Billy Graham

Every problem comes gift-wrapped in a package that also contains a creative solution. When you open the package that contains the problem, the solution is there, too. Your job is to accept both gifts.

Marie T. Freeman

Today's Integrity Builder

Today, think about the wisdom of tackling your problems sooner rather than later. Remember that "this, too, will pass," but whatever "it" is will pass more quickly if you spend more time solving your problems and less time fretting about them.

Your heart must not be troubled. Believe in God; believe also in Me.

John 14:1 Holman CSB

God is our refuge and strength, a very present help in trouble.

Psalm 46:1 NKJV

I will be with you when you pass through the waters . . . when you walk through the fire . . . the flame will not burn you. For I the Lord your God, the Holy One of Israel, and your Savior.

Isaiah 43:2-3 Holman CSB

The righteous is rescued from trouble; in his place, the wicked goes in.

Proverbs 11:8 Holman CSB

TODAY'S PRAYER

Lord, sometimes my problems are simply too big for me, but they are never too big for You. Let me turn my troubles over to You, Lord, and let me trust in You today and for all eternity. Amen

DISCIPLESHIP BUILDS CHARACTER

*He has told you men what is good and what it is the Lord
requires of you: Only to act justly, to love faithfulness,
and to walk humbly with your God.*

Micah 6:8 Holman CSB

When Jesus addressed His disciples, He warned that each one must "take up his cross and follow me." The disciples must have known exactly what the Master meant. In Jesus' day, prisoners were forced to carry their own crosses to the location where they would be put to death. Thus, Christ's message was clear: in order to follow Him, Christ's disciples must deny themselves and, instead, trust Him completely. Nothing has changed since then.

If we are to be disciples of Christ, we must trust Him and place Him at the very center of our beings. Jesus never comes "next." He is always first. The paradox, of course, is that only by sacrificing ourselves to Him do we gain salvation for ourselves.

The 19th-century writer Hannah Whitall Smith observed, "The crucial question for each of us is this: What do you think of Jesus, and do you yet have a personal acquaintance with Him?" Indeed, the answer to that question will determine the quality, the course, and the direction of your life today and for all eternity.

Jesus has called upon believers of every generation (and that includes you) to walk with Him. Jesus promises that when you follow in His footsteps, He will teach you how to live freely and lightly (Matthew 11:28-30). And when Jesus makes a promise, you can depend upon it.

There is not Christianity without a cross,
for you cannot be a disciple of Jesus
without taking up your cross.

—

Henry Blackaby

As we seek to become disciples of Jesus Christ, we should never forget that the word disciple is directly related to the word discipline. To be a disciple of the Lord Jesus Christ is to know his discipline.

Dennis Swanberg

Discipleship means allegiance to the suffering Christ, and it is therefore not at all surprising that Christians should be called upon to suffer.

Dietrich Bonhoeffer

A life lived in God is not lived on the plane of feelings, but of the will.

Elisabeth Elliot

It is not so much of our time and so much of our attention that God demands; it is not even all our time and all our attention: it is our selves.

C. S. Lewis

TODAY'S INTEGRITY BUILDER

Today, think of at least one single step that you can take to become a better disciple for Christ. Then, take that step.

Therefore, be imitators of God, as dearly loved children.

Ephesians 5:1 Holman CSB

Don't work only while being watched, in order to please men, but as slaves of Christ, do God's will from your heart. Render service with a good attitude, as to the Lord and not to men.

Ephesians 6:6-7 Holman CSB

Then Jesus said to His disciples, "If anyone wants to come with Me, he must deny himself, take up his cross, and follow Me."

Matthew 16:24 Holman CSB

And everyone who has this hope in Him purifies himself just as He is pure. Everyone who commits sin also breaks the law; sin is the breaking of law.

1 John 3:3-4 Holman CSB

TODAY'S PRAYER

Help me, Lord, to understand what cross I am to bear this day. Give me the strength and the courage to carry that cross along the path of Your choosing so that I may be a worthy disciple of Your Son. Amen

THE RIGHT PLACES, THE RIGHT FRIENDS

He who walks with wise men will be wise,
but the companion of fools will be destroyed.
Proverbs 13:20 NKJV

Whom will you try to please today: God or man? Your primary obligation, of course, is to please your Father in heaven, not your friends in the neighborhood. But even if you're a devoted Christian, you may, from time to time, feel the urge to impress your peers—and sometimes that urge can be strong.

Peer pressure can be a good thing or a bad thing, depending upon your peers. If your peers encourage you to follow God's will and to obey His commandments, then you'll experience positive peer pressure, and that's good. But, if you are involved with friends who encourage you to do foolish things, you're facing a different kind of peer pressure . . . and you'd better beware. When you feel pressured to do things—or to say things—that lead you away from God, you're aiming straight for trouble. So don't do the "easy" thing or the "popular" thing. Do the right thing, and don't worry about winning popularity contests.

Rick Warren correctly observed, "Those who follow the crowd usually get lost in it." Are you satisfied to follow that crowd? If so, you will probably pay a heavy price for your shortsightedness. But if you're determined to follow the One from Galilee, He will guide your steps and bless your undertakings. To sum it up, here's your choice: you can choose to please God first (and by doing so, strengthen your character), or you can fall prey to peer pressure. The choice is yours—and so are the consequences.

Do you want to be wise? Choose wise friends.

—

Charles Swindoll

You will get untold flak for prioritizing God's revealed and present will for your life over man's . . . but, boy, is it worth it.

Beth Moore

Comparison is the root of all feelings of inferiority.

James Dobson

It is comfortable to know that we are responsible to God and not to man. It is a small matter to be judged of man's judgement.

Lottie Moon

It is impossible to please everybody. It's not impossible to please God. So try pleasing God.

Jim Gallery

TODAY'S INTEGRITY BUILDER

When you're torn between trusting your peers or trusting your conscience, trust your conscience.

Do not be deceived: "Bad company corrupts good morals."

1 Corinthians 15:33 Holman CSB

Do not be mismatched with unbelievers. For what partnership is there between righteousness and lawlessness? Or what fellowship does light have with darkness?

2 Corinthians 6:14 Holman CSB

Dear friend, do not imitate what is evil, but what is good. The one who does good is of God; the one who does evil has not seen God.

3 John 1:11 Holman CSB

We must obey God rather than men.

Acts 5:29 Holman CSB

TODAY'S PRAYER

Dear Lord, other people may encourage me to stray from Your path, but I wish to follow in the footsteps of Your Son. Give me the vision to see the right path—and the wisdom to follow it—today and every day of my life. Amen

MATCHING YOUR ACTIONS TO YOUR BELIEFS

But be doers of the word and not hearers only.

James 1:22 Holman CSB

It takes courage to stand up for our beliefs, but it takes character to live by them. Yet far too many of us spend more energy verbalizing our beliefs than living by them—with predictable consequences.

Is your life a picture book of your creed? Are your actions congruent with your personal code? And are you willing to practice the philosophy that you preach? If so, your character will take care of itself.

But if you're doing things that don't meet with approval from the person you see in the mirror, it's time to slow down, step back, and think about how your conduct is shaping your character. If you profess to be a Christian but behave yourself as if you were not, you're living in denial. And denial, in large doses, corrodes character.

So today, make certain that your actions are guided by God's Word and by the conscience that He has placed in your heart. Don't treat your faith as if it were separate from everyday life—instead, weave your beliefs into the very fabric of your day. When you do, God will honor your good works, and your good works will honor God.

Believe and do what God says.
The life-changing consequences will be limitless,
and the results will be confidence
and peace of mind.

—

Franklin Graham

Once you have thoroughly examined your values and articulated them, you will be able to steer your life by them.

John Maxwell

God calls us to be committed to Him, to be committed to making a difference, and to be committed to reconciliation.

Bill Hybels

To believe that God—at least this God—exists is to believe that you as a person now stand in the presence of God as a Person. What would, a moment before, have been variations in opinion, now become variations in your personal attitude to a Person. You are no longer faced with an argument which demands your assent, but with a Person who demands your confidence.

C. S. Lewis

TODAY'S INTEGRITY BUILDER

Think about the importance of making your actions conform to your beliefs. Then, ask yourself if your behavior matches your rhetoric. If the answer is yes, congratulations. If not, think of a single step you can take today to stand up for the things you believe in.

Everyone who believes that Jesus is the Messiah has been born of God, and everyone who loves the parent also loves his child.

1 John 5:1 Holman CSB

I know whom I have believed and am persuaded that He is able to guard what has been entrusted to me until that day.

2 Timothy 1:12 Holman CSB

Then He said to Thomas, "Put your finger here and observe My hands. Reach out your hand and put it into My side. Don't be an unbeliever, but a believer."

John 20:27 Holman CSB

Then Jesus told the centurion, "Go. As you have believed, let it be done for you." And his servant was cured that very moment.

Matthew 8:13 Holman CSB

TODAY'S PRAYER

Heavenly Father, I believe in You, and I believe in Your Word. Help me to live in such a way that my actions validate my beliefs—and let the glory be Yours forever. Amen

WALK IN HIS TRUTH

Teach me Your way, Lord, and I will live by Your truth.
Give me an undivided mind to fear Your name.

Psalm 86:11 Holman CSB

C. H. Spurgeon observed, "Happiness is obedience, and obedience is the road to freedom." These words serve to remind us that obedience is imperative. But we live in a society that surrounds us with temptations to disobey God's laws. So if we are to win the battle against temptation and sin, we must never drop our guard.

A righteous life has many components: faith, honesty, generosity, love, kindness, humility, gratitude, and worship, to name but a few. If we seek to follow the steps of our Savior, Jesus Christ, we must seek to live according to His commandments.

When we seek righteousness in our own lives—and when we seek the companionship of likeminded friends—we not only build our characters, but we also reap the spiritual rewards that God offers those who obey Him. When we live in accordance with God's commandments, He blesses us in ways that we cannot fully understand.

Are you ready, willing, able, and anxious to receive God's blessings? Then obey Him. And rest assured that when you do your part, He'll do His part.

Don't worry about what you do not understand.
Worry about what you do understand
in the Bible but do not live by.

—

Corrie ten Boom

Faith, as Paul saw it, was a living, flaming thing leading to surrender and obedience to the commandments of Christ.

A. W. Tozer

Let us remember therefore this lesson: That to worship our God sincerely we must evermore begin by hearkening to His voice, and by giving ear to what He commands us. For if every man goes after his own way, we shall wander. We may well run, but we shall never be a whit nearer to the right way, but rather farther away from it.

John Calvin

Bible history is filled with people who began the race with great success but failed at the end because they disregarded God's rules.

Warren Wiersbe

TODAY'S INTEGRITY BUILDER

Remember this: God has given us His commandments for a reason: to obey them. These commandments are not suggestions, helpful hints, or friendly reminders—they are rules we must live by . . . or else!

Jesus answered and said unto him, If a man love me, he will keep my words: and my Father will love him, and we will come unto him, and make our abode with him.

John 14:23 KJV

Happy is the man who fears the Lord, taking great delight in His commandments.

Psalm 112:1 Holman CSB

For this is the love of God, that we keep his commandments.

1 John 5:3 KJV

Whoso despiseth the word shall be destroyed: but he that feareth the commandment shall be rewarded.

Proverbs 13:13 KJV

TODAY'S PRAYER

Thank You, Dear Lord, for loving me enough to give me rules to live by. Let me live by Your commandments, and let me lead others to do the same. Let me walk righteously in Your way, Dear Lord, this day and every day. Amen

DAY 79

CRITICS BEWARE

Don't criticize one another, brothers.
He who criticizes a brother or judges his brother criticizes
the law and judges the law. But if you judge the law,
you are not a doer of the law but a judge.

James 4:11 Holman CSB

From experience, we know that it is easier to criticize than to correct; we understand that it is easier to find faults than solutions; and we realize that excessive criticism is usually destructive, not productive. Yet the urge to criticize others remains a powerful temptation for most of us. Our task, as obedient believers, is to break the twin habits of negative thinking and critical speech.

In the book of James, we are issued a clear warning: "Don't criticize one another, brothers" (4:11 Holman CSB). Undoubtedly, James understood the paralyzing power of chronic negativity, and so must we. Negativity is highly contagious: we give it to others who, in turn, give it back to us. Thankfully, this cycle can be broken by positive thoughts, heartfelt prayers, and encouraging words.

As you examine the quality of your own communications, can you honestly say that you're a booster not a critic? If so, keep up the good words. But if you're one of those men who is occasionally overwhelmed by negativity, and if you pass that negativity along to your neighbors, it's time for a mental housecleaning.

As a thoughtful Christian, you can use the transforming power of Christ's love to break the chains of negativity. And you should.

> Being critical of others, including God,
> is one way we try to avoid facing
> and judging our own sins.
>
> —
>
> Warren Wiersbe

We shall never come to the perfect man til we come to the perfect world.

Matthew Henry

The people whom I have seen succeed best in life have always been cheerful and hopeful people who went about their business with a smile on their faces.

Charles Kingsley

The scrutiny we give other people should be for ourselves.

Oswald Chambers

TODAY'S INTEGRITY BUILDER

Negative thinking breeds more negative thinking, so nip negativity in the bud, starting today and continuing every day of your life.

TODAY'S PRAYER

Thank You, Lord, for Your infinite love. Make me an optimistic Christian, Father, as I place my hope and my trust in You. Amen

DAY 80

THE SPIRITUAL JOURNEY

*But grow in the grace and knowledge of our Lord
and Savior Jesus Christ. To Him be the glory both
now and to the day of eternity.*

2 Peter 3:18 Holman CSB

When it comes to your faith, God doesn't intend for you to stand still. He wants you to keep moving and growing. In fact, God's plan for you includes a lifetime of prayer, praise, and spiritual growth.

When we cease to grow, either emotionally or spiritually, we do ourselves and our loved ones a profound disservice. But, if we study God's Word, if we obey His commandments, and if we live in the center of His will, we will not be "stagnant" believers; we will, instead, be growing Christians . . . and that's exactly what God wants for our lives.

Many of life's most important lessons are painful to learn. During times of heartbreak and hardship, we must be courageous and we must be patient, knowing that in His own time, God will heal us if we invite Him into our hearts.

Spiritual growth need not take place only in times of adversity. We must seek to grow in our knowledge and love of the Lord every day that we live. In those quiet moments when we open our hearts to God, the One who made us keeps remaking us. He gives us direction, perspective, wisdom, and courage. The appropriate moment to accept those spiritual gifts is the present one.

Are you as mature as you're ever going to be? Hopefully not! When it comes to your faith, God doesn't intend for you to become "fully grown," at least not in this lifetime. In fact, God still has important lessons that He intends to teach you. So ask yourself this: what lesson is God trying to teach me today? And then go about the business of learning it.

The Scriptures were not given for our information,
but for our transformation.

—

D. L. Moody

There is wonderful freedom and joy in coming to recognize that the fun is in the becoming.

Gloria Gaither

Daily Bible reading is essential to victorious living and real Christian growth.

Billy Graham

Kindness in this world will do much to help others, not only to come into the light, but also to grow in grace day by day.

Fanny Crosby

The vigor of our spiritual lives will be in exact proportion to the place held by the Bible in our lives and in our thoughts.

George Mueller

Today's Integrity Builder

Times of change can be times of growth. Elisabeth Elliot reminds us that tough times can lead to a renewal of spirit: "If the leaves had not been let go to fall and wither, if the tree had not consented to be a skeleton for many months, there would be no new life rising, no bud, no flower, no fruit, no seed, no new generation." So remember: Spiritual maturity is always a journey, never a destination.

For this reason we also, since the day we heard it, do not cease to pray for you, and to ask that you may be filled with the knowledge of His will in all wisdom and spiritual understanding.

Colossians 1:9 NKJV

Therefore, leaving the elementary message about the Messiah, let us go on to maturity.

Hebrews 6:1 Holman CSB

Flee from youthful passions, and pursue righteousness, faith, love, and peace, along with those who call on the Lord from a pure heart.

2 Timothy 2:22 Holman CSB

For You, O God, have tested us; You have refined us as silver is refined. You brought us into the net; You laid affliction on our backs. You have caused men to ride over our heads; we went through fire and through water; but You brought us out to rich fulfillment.

Psalm 66:10–12 NKJV

TODAY'S PRAYER

Dear Lord, the Bible tells me that You are at work in my life, continuing to help me grow and to mature in my faith. Show me Your wisdom, Father, and let me live according to Your Word and Your will. Amen

DAY 81

BEYOND FAILURE

Peace, peace to you, and peace to him who helps you, for your God helps you.

1 Chronicles 12:18 Holman CSB

Life's occasional setbacks are simply the price that we must pay for our willingness to take risks as we follow our dreams. But even when we encounter bitter disappointments, we must never lose faith.

Hebrews 10:36 advises, "Patient endurance is what you need now, so you will continue to do God's will. Then you will receive all that he has promised" (NLT). These words remind us that when we persevere, we will eventually receive the rewards which God has promised us. What's required is perseverance, not perfection.

When we face hardships, God stands ready to protect us. Our responsibility, of course, is to ask Him for protection. When we call upon Him in heartfelt prayer, He will answer—in His own time and according to His own plan—and He will do His part to heal us. We, of course, must do our part, too.

And, while we are waiting for God's plans to unfold and for His healing touch to restore us, we can be comforted in the knowledge that our Creator can overcome any obstacle, even if we cannot.

What may seem defeat to us may be victory to him.

C. H. Spurgeon

Success or failure can be pretty well predicted by the degree to which the heart is fully in it.

John Eldredge

Never imagine that you can be a loser by trusting in God.

C. H. Spurgeon

TODAY'S INTEGRITY BUILDER

Remember that failure isn't permanent . . . unless you fail to get up. So pick yourself up, dust yourself off, and trust God. He will make it right. Warren Wiersbe had this advice: "No matter how badly we have failed, we can always get up and begin again. Our God is the God of new beginnings." And don't forget: the best time to begin again is now.

If we confess our sins, He is faithful and righteous to forgive us our sins and to cleanse us from all unrighteousness.

1 John 1:9 Holman CSB

The one who conceals his sins will not prosper, but whoever confesses and renounces them will find mercy.

Proverbs 28:13 Holman CSB

An ear that listens to life-giving rebukes will be at home among the wise.

Proverbs 15:31 Holman CSB

Therefore we do not give up; even though our outer person is being destroyed, our inner person is being renewed day by day.

2 Corinthians 4:16 Holman CSB

TODAY'S PRAYER

Dear Lord, when I encounter failures and disappointments, keep me mindful that You are in control. Let me persevere—even if my soul is troubled—and let me follow Your Son, Jesus Christ, this day and forever. Amen

DAY 82

BUILDING CHARACTER IN SILENCE

*I sought the Lord, and He heard me,
and delivered me from all my fears.*

Psalm 34:4 NKJV

Here's a simple little prescription for character-building: carve out a little time for silence every day.

Here in our noisy, 21st-century world, silence is highly underrated. Many of us can't even seem to walk from the front door to the street without a cell phone or an iPod in our ear. The world seems to grow louder day by day, and our senses seem to be invaded at every turn. But, if we allow the distractions of a clamorous society to separate us from God's peace, we do ourselves a profound disservice. So if we're wise, we make time each day for quiet reflection. And when we do, we are rewarded.

Are you a man who takes time each day for an extended period of silence? And during those precious moments, do you sincerely open your heart to your Creator? If so, you will be blessed. If not, then the struggles and stresses of everyday living may rob you of the peace that should rightfully be yours because of your personal relationship with Christ. So take time each day to quietly commune with your Creator. When you do, those moments of silence will enable you to participate more fully in the only source of peace that endures: God's peace.

Silence is as fit a garment for devotion
as any other language.

—

C. H. Spurgeon

If the pace and the push, the noise and the crowds are getting to you, it's time to stop the nonsense and find a place of solace to refresh your spirit.

Charles Swindoll

The remedy for distractions is the same now as it was in earlier and simpler times: prayer, meditation, and the cultivation of the inner life.

A. W. Tozer

Growth takes place in quietness, in hidden ways, in silence and solitude. The process is not accessible to observation.

Eugene Peterson

The Lord Jesus, available to people much of the time, left them, sometimes a great while before day, to go up to the hills where He could commune in solitude with His Father.

Elisabeth Elliot

TODAY'S INTEGRITY BUILDER

Want to talk to God? Then don't make Him shout. If you really want to hear from God, go to a quiet place and listen. If you keep listening long enough and carefully enough, He'll start talking.

Be still, and know that I am God.

Psalm 46:10 NKJV

Be silent before the Lord and wait expectantly for Him.

Psalm 37:7 Holman CSB

In quietness and confidence shall be your strength.

Isaiah 30:15 NKJV

I am not alone, because the Father is with Me.

John 16:32 Holman CSB

TODAY'S PRAYER

Dear Lord, in the quiet moments of this day, I will turn my thoughts and prayers to You. In silence I will sense Your presence, and I will seek Your will for my life, knowing that when I accept Your peace, I will be blessed today and throughout eternity. Amen

HE WANTS TO TEACH

He awakens [Me] each morning; He awakens My ear to listen like those being instructed. The Lord God has opened My ear, and I was not rebellious; I did not turn back.

Isaiah 50:4-5 Holman CSB

The Bible promises that God will guide you if you let Him. Your job, of course, is to let Him. But sometimes, you will be tempted to do otherwise. Sometimes, you'll be tempted to go along with the crowd; other times, you'll be tempted to do things your way, not God's way. When you feel those temptations, you must resist them, or else.

What will you allow to guide you through the coming day: your own desires (or, for that matter, the desires of your peers)? Or will you allow God to lead the way? The answer should be obvious. You should let God be your guide. When you entrust your life to Him completely and without reservation, God will give you the strength to meet any challenge, the courage to face any trial, and the wisdom to live in His righteousness. So trust Him today and seek His guidance. When you do, your character will most certainly take care of itself, and your next step will most assuredly be the right one.

Fix your eyes upon the Lord! Do it once. Do it daily. Do it constantly. Look at the Lord and keep looking at Him.

Charles Swindoll

God's plan for our guidance is for us to grow gradually in wisdom before we get to the crossroads.

Bill Hybels

Are you serious about wanting God's guidance to become a personal reality in your life? The first step is to tell God that you know you can't manage your own life; that you need his help.

Catherine Marshall

We must always invite Jesus to be the navigator of our plans, desires, wills, and emotions, for He is the way, the truth, and the life.

Bill Bright

TODAY'S INTEGRITY BUILDER

Would you like God's guidance? Then ask Him for it. When you pray for guidance, God will give it (Luke 11:9). So ask.

In all your ways acknowledge Him, and He shall direct your paths.

Proverbs 3:6 NKJV

Yet Lord, You are our Father; we are the clay, and You are our potter; we all are the work of Your hands.

Isaiah 64:8 Holman CSB

Lord, You are my lamp; the Lord illuminates my darkness.

2 Samuel 22:29 Holman CSB

TODAY'S PRAYER

Dear Lord, thank You for Your constant presence and Your constant love. I draw near to You this day with the confidence that You are ready to guide me. Help me walk closely with You, Father, and help me share Your Good News with all who cross my path. Amen

LOVE IS A CHOICE

No one has greater love than this,
that someone would lay down his life for his friends.

John 15:13 Holman CSB

L ove is a choice. Either you choose to behave lovingly toward others . . . or not; either you behave yourself in ways that enhance your relationships . . . or not. But make no mistake: genuine love requires effort. Simply put, if you wish to build lasting relationships, you must be willing to do your part.

Since the days of Adam and Eve, God has allowed His children to make choices for themselves, and so it is with you. As you interact with family and friends, you have choices to make . . . lots of them. If you choose wisely, you'll be rewarded; if you choose unwisely, you'll bear the consequences.

Christ's words are clear: we are to love God first, and secondly, we are to love others as we love ourselves (Matthew 22:37-40). These two commands are seldom easy, and because we are imperfect beings, we often fall short. But God's Holy Word commands us to try.

The Christian path is an exercise in love and forgiveness. If we are to walk in Christ's footsteps, we must forgive those who have done us harm, and we must accept Christ's love by sharing it freely with family, friends, neighbors, and even strangers.

God does not intend for you to experience mediocre relationships; He created you for far greater things. Building lasting relationships requires compassion, wisdom, empathy, kindness, courtesy, and forgiveness. If that sounds a lot like work, it is—which is perfectly fine with God. Why? Because He knows that you are capable of doing that work, and because He knows that the fruits of your labors will enrich the lives of your loved ones and the lives of generations yet unborn.

Homes that are built on anything
other than love are bound to crumble.

—

Billy Graham

Sacrificial love, giving-up love, is love that is willing to go to any lengths to provide for the well-being of the beloved.

Ed Young

It is when we come to the Lord in our nothingness, our powerlessness and our helplessness that He then enables us to love in a way which, without Him, would be absolutely impossible.

Elisabeth Elliot

Suppose that I understand the Bible. And, suppose that I am the greatest preacher who ever lived! The Apostle Paul wrote that unless I have love, "I am nothing."

Billy Graham

Faith, like light, should always be simple and unbending; love, like warmth, should beam forth on every side and bend to every necessity of our brethren.

Martin Luther

TODAY'S INTEGRITY BUILDER

Do you want love to last? Then you must understand this: Genuine love requires effort. That's why those who are lazy in love are often losers in love, too!

Though I speak with the tongues of men and of angels, but have not love, I have become sounding brass or a clanging cymbal.

1 Corinthians 13:1 NKJV

Dear friends, if God loved us in this way, we also must love one another.

1 John 4:11 Holman CSB

Love one another earnestly from a pure heart.

1 Peter 1:22 Holman CSB

Above all, keep your love for one another at full strength, since love covers a multitude of sins.

1 Peter 4:8 Holman CSB

TODAY'S PRAYER

Lord, You have given me the gift of love and You've asked me to share it. The gift of love is a precious gift indeed. Let me nurture love and treasure it. And, help me remember that the essence of love is not to receive it, but to give it, today and forever. Amen

DAY 85

GOT STRENGTH?

God, create a clean heart for me
and renew a steadfast spirit within me.
Psalm 51:10 Holman CSB

E ven the most inspired Christian men can, from time to time, find themselves running on empty. The demands of daily life can drain us of our strength and rob us of the joy that is rightfully ours in Christ. When we find ourselves tired, discouraged, or worse, there is a source from which we can draw the power needed to recharge our spiritual batteries. That source is God.

God intends that His children lead joyous lives filled with abundance and peace. But sometimes, abundance and peace seem very far away. It is then that we must turn to God for renewal, and when we do, He will restore us if we allow Him to do so.

Today, like every other day, is literally brimming with possibilities. Whether we realize it or not, God is always working in us and through us; our job is to let Him do His work without undue interference. Yet we are imperfect beings who, because of our limited vision, often resist God's will. And oftentimes, because of our stubborn insistence on squeezing too many activities into a 24-hour day, we allow ourselves to become exhausted, or frustrated, or both.

Are you tired or troubled? Turn your heart toward God in prayer. Are you weak or worried? Take the time—or, more accurately, make the time—to delve deeply into God's Holy Word. Are you spiritually depleted? Call upon fellow believers to support you, and call upon Christ to renew your spirit and your life. Are you simply overwhelmed by the demands of the day? Pray for the wisdom to simplify your life. Are you exhausted? Pray for the wisdom to rest a little more and worry a little less.

When you do these things, you'll discover that the Creator of the universe stands always ready and always able to create a new sense of wonderment and joy in you.

The resurrection of Jesus Christ is the power of God to change history and to change lives.

—

Bill Bright

Walking with God leads to receiving his intimate counsel, and counseling leads to deep restoration.

John Eldredge

One reason so much American Christianity is a mile wide and an inch deep is that Christians are simply tired. Sometimes you need to kick back and rest for Jesus' sake.

Dennis Swanberg

Notice what Jesus had to say concerning those who have wearied themselves by trying to do things in their own strength: "Come to me, all you who labor and are heavy laden, and I will give you rest."

Henry Blackaby and Claude King

A divine strength is given to those who yield themselves to the Father and obey what He tells them to do.

Warren Wiersbe

TODAY'S INTEGRITY BUILDER

Need strength? Let God's spirit reign over your heart: Anne Graham Lotz writes, "The amount of power you experience to live a victorious, triumphant Christian life is directly proportional to the freedom you give the Spirit to be Lord of your life!" And remember that the best time to begin living triumphantly is the present moment.

And He said to me, "My grace is sufficient for you, for My strength is made perfect in weakness."

2 Corinthians 12:9 NKJV

You, therefore, my child, be strong in the grace that is in Christ Jesus.

2 Timothy 2:1 Holman CSB

The Lord is my strength and my song; He has become my salvation.

Exodus 15:2 Holman CSB

He gives strength to the weary and strengthens the powerless.

Isaiah 40:29 Holman CSB

TODAY'S PRAYER

Dear Lord, sometimes the demands of the day leave me discouraged and frustrated. Renew my strength, Father, and give me patience and perspective. Today and every day, let me draw comfort and courage from Your promises, from Your love, and from Your Son. Amen

OBSERVING THE SABBATH

Remember the Sabbath day, to keep it holy.

Exodus 20:8 NKJV

Whom God gave Moses the Ten Commandments, it became perfectly clear that our Heavenly Father intends for us to make the Sabbath a holy day, a day for worship, for contemplation, for fellowship, and for rest. Yet we live in a seven-day-a-week world, a world that all too often treats Sunday as a regular workday.

One way to strengthen your character is by giving God at least one day each week. If you carve out the time for a day of worship and praise, you'll be amazed at the impact it will have on the rest of your week. But if you fail to honor God's day, if you treat the Sabbath as a day to work or a day to party, you'll miss out on a harvest of blessings that is only available one day each week.

How does your family observe the Lord's day? When church is over, do you treat Sunday like any other day of the week? If so, it's time to think long and hard about your family's schedule and your family's priorities. And if you've been treating Sunday as just another day, it's time to break that habit. When Sunday rolls around, don't try to fill every spare moment. Take time to rest . . . Father's orders!

God asks that we worship Him with our concentrated
minds as well as with our wills and emotions.
A divided and scattered mind is not effective.

—

Catherine Marshall

Worship is not taught from the pulpit. It must be learned in the heart.

Jim Elliot

Worship is a daunting task. Each worships differently. But each should worship.

Max Lucado

There is no division into sacred and secular; it is all one great, glorious life.

Oswald Chambers

TODAY'S INTEGRITY BUILDER

Today, think about new ways that you can honor God on the Sabbath. The Sabbath is unlike the other six days of the week, and it's up to you to treat it that way.

TODAY'S PRAYER

Dear Lord, I thank You for the Sabbath day, a day when my family and I can worship You and praise Your Son. We will keep the Sabbath as a holy day, a day when we can honor You. Amen

THE KEY TO SUCCESS: DON'T TIRE OF DOING THE RIGHT THING

So we must not get tired of doing good,
for we will reap at the proper time if we don't give up.

Galatians 6:9 Holman CSB

Would you like a time-tested formula for successful living? Here is a formula that is proven and true: Seek God's approval in every aspect of your life. Does this sound too simple? Perhaps it is simple, but it is also the only way to reap the marvelous riches that God has in store for you.

So today, take every step of your journey with God as your traveling companion. Read His Word and follow His commandments. Support only those activities that further God's kingdom and your spiritual growth. Be an example of righteous living to your friends, to your neighbors, and to your children. Then, reap the blessings that God has promised to all those who live according to His will and His Word.

The best evidence of our having the truth is our walking in the truth.

Matthew Henry

If we have the true love of God in our hearts, we will show it in our lives. We will not have to go up and down the earth proclaiming it. We will show it in everything we say or do.

D. L. Moody

The purity of motive determines the quality of action.

Oswald Chambers

Righteousness comes only from God.

Kay Arthur

We pursue righteousness when we flee the things that keep us from following the Lord Jesus. These are the keys: flee, follow, and fight.

Franklin Graham

TODAY'S INTEGRITY BUILDER

Today, consider the value of living a life that is pleasing to God. And while you're at it, think about the rewards that are likely to be yours when you do the right thing day in and day out.

For the eyes of the Lord are over the righteous, and his ears are open unto their prayers: but the face of the Lord is against them that do evil.

1 Peter 3:12 KJV

Blessed are the pure in heart, for they shall see God.

Matthew 5:8 NKJV

But seek first the kingdom of God and His righteousness, and all these things will be provided for you.

Matthew 6:33 Holman CSB

When I am filled with cares, Your comfort brings me joy.

Psalm 94:19 Holman CSB

TODAY'S PRAYER

Holy Father, let my thoughts and my deeds be pleasing to You. I thank You, Lord, for Jesus. Today and every day, I will follow in His footsteps so that my life can be a living testimony to Your love, to Your forgiveness, and to Your Son. Amen

ACKNOWLEDGING HIS PRESENCE BUILDS CHARACTER

Draw near to God, and He will draw near to you.

James 4:8 Holman CSB

In the quiet early morning, as the sun's first rays peak over the horizon, we may sense the presence of God. But as the day wears on and the demands of everyday life bear down upon us, we may become so wrapped up in earthly concerns that we forget to praise the Creator.

God is everywhere we have ever been and everywhere we will ever be. When we turn to Him often, we are blessed by His presence. But, if we ignore God's presence or rebel against it altogether, the world in which we live soon becomes a spiritual wasteland.

Since God is everywhere, we are free to sense His presence whenever we take the time to quiet our souls and turn our prayers to Him. But sometimes, amid the incessant demands of everyday life, we turn our thoughts far from God; when we do, we suffer.

Are you tired, discouraged or fearful? Be comforted because God is with you. Are you confused? Listen to the quiet voice of your Heavenly Father. Are you bitter? Talk with God and seek His guidance. Are you celebrating a great victory? Thank God and praise Him. He is the Giver of all things good. In whatever condition you find yourself—whether you are happy or sad, victorious or vanquished, troubled or triumphant—celebrate God's presence. And be comforted in the knowledge that God is not just near. He is here.

No matter what trials we face, Christ never leaves us.

—

Billy Graham

There is a basic urge: the longing for unity. You desire a reunion with God—with God your Father.

E. Stanley Jones

The next time you hear a baby laugh or see an ocean wave, take note. Pause and listen as his Majesty whispers ever so gently, "I'm here."

Max Lucado

The real test of being in the presence of God is that you either forget about yourself altogether or see yourself as a very small object. It is better to forget about yourself altogether.

C. S. Lewis

Get yourself into the presence of the loving Father. Just place yourself before Him, and look up into His face; think of His love, His wonderful, tender, pitying love.

Andrew Murray

TODAY'S INTEGRITY BUILDER

Having trouble hearing God? If so, slow yourself down, tune out the distractions, and listen carefully. God has important things to say; your task is to be still and listen.

Now he who keeps His commandments abides in Him, and He in him. And by this we know that He abides in us, by the Spirit whom He has given us.

1 John 3:24 NKJV

For the eyes of the Lord range throughout the earth to show Himself strong for those whose hearts are completely His.

2 Chronicles 16:9 Holman CSB

From one man He has made every nation of men to live all over the earth and has determined their appointed times and the boundaries of where they live, so that they might seek God, and perhaps they might reach out and find Him, though He is not far from each one of us.

Acts 17:26-27 Holman CSB

You will seek Me and find Me when you search for Me with all your heart.

Jeremiah 29:13 Holman CSB

TODAY'S PRAYER

Dear Lord, You are with me always. Help me feel Your presence in every situation and every circumstance. Today, Dear God, let me feel You and acknowledge Your presence, Your love, and Your Son. Amen

DAY 89

OVERCOMING ADDICTION BUILDS CHARACTER

Be sober! Be on the alert!
Your adversary the Devil is prowling around like
a roaring lion, looking for anyone he can devour.
1 Peter 5:8 Holman CSB

If you'd like a perfect formula for character destruction, here it is: become addicted to something that destroys your health or your sanity. If (God forbid) you allow yourself to become addicted, you're steering straight for a tidal wave of negative consequences, and fast.

Ours is a society that glamorizes the use of drugs, alcohol, cigarettes, and other addictive substances. Why? The answer can be summed up in one word: money. Simply put, addictive substances are big money makers, so suppliers (of both legal and illegal substances) work overtime to make certain that people like you sample their products. The suppliers need a steady stream of new customers because the old ones are dying off (fast), so they engage in a no-holds-barred struggle to find new users—or more accurately, new abusers.

The dictionary defines addiction as "the compulsive need for a habit-forming substance; the condition of being habitually and compulsively occupied with something." That definition is accurate, but incomplete. For Christians, addiction has an additional meaning: it means compulsively worshipping something other than God.

Unless you're living on a deserted island, you know people who are full-blown addicts—probably lots of people. If you, or someone you love, is suffering from the blight of addiction, remember this: Help is available. Plenty of people have experienced addiction and lived to tell about it . . . so don't give up hope.

And if you're one of those fortunate people who hasn't started experimenting with addictive substances, congratulations! You have just spared yourself a lifetime of headaches and heartaches.

> Since behaviors become habits,
> make them work with you and not against you.
>
> —
>
> E. Stanley Jones

We are meant to be addicted to God, but we develop secondary addictions that temporarily appear to fix our problem.

Edward M. Berckman

Addiction is the most powerful psychic enemy of humanity's desire for God.

Gerald May

Above all, we must be especially alert against the beginnings of temptation, for the enemy is more easily conquered if he is refused admittance to the mind and is met beyond the threshold when he knocks.

Thomas à Kempis

A man may not be responsible for his last drink, but he certainly was for the first.

Billy Graham

TODAY'S INTEGRITY BUILDER

Remember that ultimately you and you alone are responsible for controlling your appetites. Others may warn you, help you, or encourage you, but in the end, the habits that rule your life are the very same habits that you yourself have formed. Thankfully, since you formed these habits, you can also break them—if you decide to do so.

You shall have no other gods before Me.

Exodus 20:3 NKJV

For we do not have a High Priest who cannot sympathize with our weaknesses, but was in all points tempted as we are, yet without sin. Let us therefore come boldly to the throne of grace, that we may obtain mercy and find grace to help in time of need.

Hebrews 4:15-16 NKJV

Jesus responded, "I assure you: Everyone who commits sin is a slave of sin."

John 8:34 Holman CSB

Yet in all these things we are more than conquerors through Him who loved us.

Romans 8:37 NKJV

TODAY'S PRAYER

Dear Lord, You have instructed me to care for my body, and I will obey You. I will be mindful of the destructive power of addiction, and I will avoid the people, the places, and the substances that can entrap my spirit and destroy my life. Amen

HARD WORK BUILDS INTEGRITY

Do not lack diligence; be fervent in spirit; serve the Lord.
Romans 12:11 Holman CSB

The old adage is both familiar and true: We must pray as if everything depended upon God, but work as if everything depended upon us. Yet sometimes, when we are weary and discouraged, we may allow our worries to sap our energy and our hope. God has other intentions. God intends that we pray for things, and He intends that we be willing to work for the things that we pray for. More importantly, God intends that our work should become His work.

Whether you're in school or in the workplace, your success will depend, in large part, upon the passion that you bring to your work. God has created a world in which diligence is rewarded and sloth is not. So whatever you choose to do, do it with commitment, with excitement, with enthusiasm, and with vigor.

In his second letter to the Thessalonians, Paul warns, ". . . if any would not work, neither should he eat" (3:10 KJV). And the Book of Proverbs proclaims, "One who is slack in his work is brother to one who destroys" (18:9 NIV). Clearly, God's Word commends the value and importance of diligence. Yet we live in a world that, all too often, glorifies leisure while downplaying the importance of shoulder-to-the wheel hard work. Rest assured, however, that God does not underestimate the value of diligence. And neither should you.

It has been said that there are no shortcuts to any place worth going. And for believers, it's important to remember that hard work is not simply a proven way to get ahead, it's also part of God's plan for His children.

God did not create you to be ordinary; He created you for far greater things. Reaching for greater things usually requires work and lots of it, which is perfectly fine with God. After all, He knows that you're up to the task, and He has big plans for you. Very big plans.

If you want to reach your potential,
you need to add a strong work ethic to your talent.

—

John Maxwell

Chiefly the mold of a man's fortune is in his own hands.

Francis Bacon

Thank God every morning when you get up that you have something which must be done, whether you like it or not. Work breeds a hundred virtues that idleness never knows.

Charles Kingsley

The world does not consider labor a blessing, therefore it flees and hates it, but the pious who fear the Lord labor with a ready and cheerful heart, for they know God's command, and they acknowledge His calling.

Martin Luther

People who work for money only are usually miserable, because there is no fulfillment and no meaning to what they do.

Dave Ramsey

TODAY'S INTEGRITY BUILDER

Here's a time-tested formula for success: have faith in God and do the work. It has been said that there are no shortcuts to any place worth going. Hard work is not simply a proven way to get ahead, it's also part of God's plan for all His children (including you).

Whatever you do, do it enthusiastically, as something done for the Lord and not for men.

Colossians 3:23 Holman CSB

Be strong and courageous, and do the work. Don't be afraid or discouraged, for the Lord God, my God, is with you. He won't leave you or forsake you.

1 Chronicles 28:20 Holman CSB

But thanks be to God, who gives us the victory through our Lord Jesus Christ. Therefore, my beloved brethren, be steadfast, immovable, always abounding in the work of the Lord, knowing that your labor is not in vain in the Lord.

1 Corinthians 15:57-58 NKJV

Now the one who plants and the one who waters are equal, and each will receive his own reward according to his own labor.

1 Corinthians 3:8 Holman CSB

TODAY'S PRAYER

Lord, let me be an industrious worker in Your fields. Those fields are ripe, Lord, and Your workers are few. Let me be counted as Your faithful, diligent servant today, and every day. Amen

DAY 91

BUILDING CHARACTER BY FINDING COURAGE

Be strong and courageous, and do the work.
Don't be afraid or discouraged, for the Lord God, my God,
is with you. He won't leave you or forsake you.

1 Chronicles 28:20 Holman CSB

Courage builds character and vice versa. So if you'd like a brief course in character-building, try this: the next time you face a choice between doing the right thing or the easy thing, summon the courage to do the right thing. And while you're summoning that courage, ask God to help.

Billy Graham observed, "Down through the centuries, in times of trouble and trial, God has brought courage to the hearts of those who love Him. The Bible is filled with assurances of God's help and comfort in every kind of trouble which might cause fears to arise in the human heart. You can look ahead with promise, hope, and joy." Dr. Graham's words apply to you.

The next time you find your courage tested by the inevitable challenges of life, remember that God is as near as your next breath. He is your shield and your strength; He is your protector and your deliverer. Call upon Him in your hour of need and then be comforted. Whatever your challenge, whatever your trouble, God can handle it. And will.

Are you fearful? First, bow your head and pray for God's strength. Then, raise your head knowing that, together, you and God can handle whatever comes your way.

—

Jim Gallery

Take courage. We walk in the wilderness today and in the Promised Land tomorrow.

D. L. Moody

What is courage? It is the ability to be strong in trust, in conviction, in obedience. To be courageous is to step out in faith—to trust and obey, no matter what.

Kay Arthur

Courage is not simply one of the virtues, but the form of every virtue at the testing point, which means, at the point of highest reality. A chastity or honesty or mercy which yields to danger will be chaste or honest or merciful only on conditions. Pilate was merciful till it became risky.

C. S. Lewis

The fear of God is the death of every other fear.

C. H. Spurgeon

TODAY'S INTEGRITY BUILDER

Is your courage being tested today? Cling tightly to God's promises, and pray. God can give you the strength to meet any challenge, and that's exactly what you should ask Him to do.

The Lord is the One who will go before you. He will be with you; He will not leave you or forsake you. Do not be afraid or discouraged.

Deuteronomy 31:8 Holman CSB

Do not fear, for I am with you; do not be afraid, for I am your God. I will strengthen you; I will help you; I will hold on to you with My righteous right hand.

Isaiah 41:10 Holman CSB

Peace I leave with you, my peace I give unto you: not as the world giveth, give I unto you. Let not your heart be troubled, neither let it be afraid.

John 14:27 KJV

In thee, O Lord, do I put my trust; let me never be put into confusion.

Psalm 71:1 KJV

TODAY'S PRAYER

Lord, at times, this world is a fearful place. I fear for my family and especially for my children. Yet, You have promised me that You are with me always. With You as my protector, I am not afraid. Today, Dear Lord, let me live courageously as I place my trust in You. Amen

DAY 92

GRATITUDE BUILDS CHARACTER

In everything give thanks;
for this is the will of God in Christ Jesus for you.
1 Thessalonians 5:18 NKJV

As Christians, we are blessed beyond measure. God sent His only Son to die for our sins. And, God has given us the priceless gifts of eternal love and eternal life. We, in turn, are instructed to approach our Heavenly Father with reverence and thanksgiving. But sometimes, in the crush of everyday living, we simply don't stop long enough to pause and thank our Creator for the countless blessings He has bestowed upon us.

When we slow down and express our gratitude to the One who made us, we enrich our own lives and the lives of those around us. Thanksgiving should become a habit, a regular part of our daily routines. God has blessed us beyond measure, and we owe Him everything, including our eternal praise.

Are you a thankful person? Do you appreciate the gifts that God has given you? And, do you demonstrate your gratitude by being a faithful steward of the gifts and talents that you have received from your Creator? You most certainly should be thankful. After all, when you stop to think about it, God has given you more blessings than you can count. So the question of the day is this: will you thank your Heavenly Father . . . or will you spend your time and energy doing other things?

God is always listening—are you willing to say thanks? It's up to you, and the next move is yours.

It is only with gratitude that life becomes rich.

—

Dietrich Bonhoeffer

We ought to give thanks for all fortune: if it is good, because it is good, if bad, because it works in us patience, humility, and the contempt of this world along with the hope of our eternal country.

C. S. Lewis

The words "thank" and "think" come from the same root word. If we would think more, we would thank more.

Warren Wiersbe

Think of the blessings we so easily take for granted: Life itself; preservation from danger; every bit of health we enjoy; every hour of liberty; the ability to see, to hear, to speak, to think, and to imagine all this comes from the hand of God.

Billy Graham

A spirit of thankfulness makes all the difference.

Billy Graham

TODAY'S INTEGRITY BUILDER

Since you're thankful to God, tell Him so. And keep telling Him so every day of your life.

Thanks be to God for His indescribable gift.

2 Corinthians 9:15 Holman CSB

Therefore as you have received Christ Jesus the Lord, walk in Him, rooted and built up in Him and established in the faith, just as you were taught, and overflowing with thankfulness.

Colossians 2:6-7 Holman CSB

Enter into His gates with thanksgiving, and into His courts with praise. Be thankful to Him, and bless His name. For the Lord is good; His mercy is everlasting, and His truth endures to all generations.

Psalm 100:4-5 NKJV

And whatever you do, in word or in deed, do everything in the name of the Lord Jesus, giving thanks to God the Father through Him.

Colossians 3:17 Holman CSB

TODAY'S PRAYER

Lord, You have blessed me with a loving family—make me a father who is thankful, loving, responsible, and wise. I praise You, Father, for the gift of Your Son and for the gift of salvation. Let me be a joyful Christian and a worthy example, this day and every day that I live. Amen

HOLDING ON TO HOPE

We have this hope—like a sure and firm anchor of the soul—
that enters the inner sanctuary behind the curtain.

Hebrews 6:19 Holman CSB

There are few sadder sights on earth than the sight of a man or woman who has lost all hope. In difficult times, hope can be elusive, but those who place their faith in God's promises need never lose it. After all, God is good; His love endures; He has promised His children the gift of eternal life. And, God keeps His promises.

Despite God's promises, despite Christ's love, and despite our countless blessings, we frail human beings can still lose hope from time to time. When we do, we need the encouragement of Christian friends, the life-changing power of prayer, and the healing truth of God's Holy Word.

If you find yourself falling into the spiritual traps of worry and discouragement, seek the healing touch of Jesus and the encouraging words of fellow Christians. If you find a friend in need, remind him or her of the peace that is found through a personal relationship with Christ. It was Christ who promised, "These things I have spoken unto you, that in me ye might have peace. In the world ye shall have tribulation: but be of good cheer; I have overcome the world" (John 16:33 KJV). This world can be a place of trials and tribulations, but as believers, we are secure. God has promised us peace, joy, and eternal life. And, of course, God keeps His promises today, tomorrow, and forever.

The hope we have in Jesus is the anchor for the soul—
something sure and steadfast, preventing drifting or
giving way, lowered to the depth of God's love.

—

Franklin Graham

Faith looks back and draws courage; hope looks ahead and keeps desire alive.

John Eldredge

If your hopes are being disappointed just now, it means that they are being purified.

Oswald Chambers

Down through the centuries in times of trouble and trial, God has brought courage to the hearts of those who love Him. The Bible is filled with assurances of God's help and comfort in every kind of trouble which might cause fears to arise in the human heart. You can look ahead with promise, hope, and joy.

Billy Graham

TODAY'S INTEGRITY BUILDER

If you're experiencing hard times, you'll be wise to start spending more time with God. And if you do your part, God will do His part. So never be afraid to hope—or to ask—for a miracle.

Let us hold on to the confession of our hope without wavering, for He who promised is faithful.

Hebrews 10:23 Holman CSB

For in You, O Lord, I hope; You will hear, O Lord my God.

Psalm 38:15 NKJV

The Lord is good to those who wait for Him, to the person who seeks Him.

Lamentations 3:25 Holman CSB

Now may the God of hope fill you with all joy and peace in believing, so that you may overflow with hope by the power of the Holy Spirit.

Romans 15:13 Holman CSB

TODAY'S PRAYER

Dear Lord, make me a man of hope. If I become discouraged, let me turn to You. If I grow weary, let me seek strength in You. When I face adversity, let me seek Your will and trust Your Word. In every aspect of my life, I will trust You, Father, so that my heart will be filled with faith and hope, this day and forever. Amen

DAY 94

THE RIGHT KIND OF FEAR

Better a little with the fear of the Lord
than great treasure with turmoil.

Proverbs 15:16 Holman CSB

D o you possesses a healthy, fearful respect for God's power? Hopefully so. After all, the lesson from the Book of Proverbs is clear: "The fear of the Lord is the beginning of knowledge, but fools despise wisdom and instruction" (1:7 NKJV). Yet, you live in a world that often ignores the role that God plays in shaping the affairs of mankind. You live in a world where too many people consider it "unfashionable" or "unseemly" to discuss the fear of God. Don't count yourself among their number.

To fear God is to acknowledge His sovereignty over every aspect of His creation (including you). To fear God is to place your relationship with God in its proper perspective (He is your master; you are His servant). To fear God is to dread the very thought of disobeying Him. To fear God is to humble yourself in the presence of His infinite power and His infinite love.

God praises humility and punishes pride. That's why God's greatest servants will always be those humble men and women who care less for their own glory and more for God's glory. In God's kingdom, the only way to achieve greatness is to shun it. And the only way to be wise is to understand these facts: God is great; He is all-knowing; and He is all-powerful. We must respect Him, and we must humbly obey His commandments, or we must accept the consequences of our misplaced pride.

When we fear the Creator—and when we honor Him by obeying His teachings—we receive God's approval and His blessings. But, when we ignore Him or disobey His commandments, we invite disastrous consequences.

The fear of the Lord is, indeed, the beginning of knowledge. So today, as you face the realities of everyday life, remember this: until you acquire a healthy, respectful fear of God's power, your education is incomplete, and so is your faith.

The fear of God is the death of every other fear.

—

C. H. Spurgeon

The remarkable thing about fearing God is that when you fear God, you fear nothing else, whereas if you do not fear God, you fear everything else.

Oswald Chambers

A healthy fear of God will do much to deter us from sin.

Charles Swindoll

It is not possible that mortal men should be thoroughly conscious of the divine presence without being filled with awe.

C. H. Spurgeon

Remember that this fear of the Lord is His treasure, a choice jewel, given only to favorites, and to those who are greatly beloved.

John Bunyan

TODAY'S INTEGRITY BUILDER

Ask yourself this question: how fearful are you of disobeying God? If the answer is "a lot," you win the prize. But if the honest answer is "not much," then spend a few moments thinking about the potential consequences—perhaps disastrous consequences—that might result from your disobedience.

Don't consider yourself to be wise; fear the Lord and turn away from evil.

Proverbs 3:7 Holman CSB

The fear of the Lord is the beginning of knowledge, but fools despise wisdom and instruction.

Proverbs 1:7 NKJV

To fear the Lord is to hate evil.

Proverbs 8:13 Holman CSB

The fear of the Lord is the beginning of wisdom, and the knowledge of the Holy One is understanding.

Proverbs 9:10 Holman CSB

TODAY'S PRAYER

Lord, You love me and protect me. I praise You, Father, for Your grace, and I respect You for Your infinite power. Let my greatest fear in life be the fear of displeasing You. Amen

LISTEN CAREFULLY TO GOD

The one who is from God listens to God's words.
This is why you don't listen, because you are not from God.

John 8:47 Holman CSB

Sometimes God speaks loudly and clearly. More often, He speaks in a quiet voice—and if you are wise, you will be listening carefully when He does. To do so, you must carve out quiet moments each day to study His Word and sense His direction. And you can be sure that every time you listen to God, you will receive lessons a in character-building.

Can you quiet yourself long enough to listen to your conscience? Are you attuned to the subtle guidance of your intuition? Are you willing to pray sincerely and then to wait quietly for God's response? Hopefully so, because the more carefully you listen to your Creator, the more He will work in you and through you.

Usually God refrains from sending His messages on stone tablets or city billboards. More often, He communicates in subtler ways. If you sincerely desire to hear His voice (and strengthen your character), you must listen carefully, and you must do so in the silent corners of your quiet, willing heart.

In the soul-searching of our lives, we are to stay quiet so we can hear Him say all that He wants to say to us in our hearts.

Charles Swindoll

An essential condition of listening to God is that the mind should not be distracted by thoughts of resentment, ill-temper, hatred or vengeance, all of which are comprised in the general term, the wrath of man.

R. V. G. Tasker

TODAY'S INTEGRITY BUILDER

Today, take a few moments to consider the fact that prayer is two-way communication with God. Talking to God isn't enough; you should also listen to Him.

TODAY'S PRAYER

Lord, give me the wisdom to be a good listener. Help me listen carefully to my family, to my friends, and—most importantly—to You. Amen

REAL REPENTANCE BUILDS CHARACTER

The one who conceals his sins will not prosper,
but whoever confesses and renounces them will find mercy.

Proverbs 28:13 Holman CSB

Who among us has sinned? All of us. But, God calls upon us to turn away from sin by following His commandments. And the good news is this: When we do ask God's forgiveness and turn our hearts to Him, He forgives us absolutely and completely.

Genuine repentance requires more than simply offering God apologies for our misdeeds. Real repentance may start with feelings of sorrow and remorse, but it ends only when we turn away from the sin that has heretofore distanced us from our Creator. In truth, we offer our most meaningful apologies to God not with our words, but with our actions. As long as we are still engaged in sin, we may be "repenting," but we have not fully "repented."

Is there an aspect of your life that is distancing you from your God? If so, ask for His forgiveness, and—just as importantly—stop sinning. Then, wrap yourself in the protection of God's Word. When you do, both you and your character will be secure.

But suppose we do sin. Suppose we slip and fall. Suppose we yield to temptation for a moment. What happens? We have to confess that sin.

Billy Graham

Ten thousand confessions, if they do not spring from really contrite hearts, shall only be additions to their guilt.

C. H. Spurgeon

Repentance involves a radical change of heart and mind in which we agree with God's evaluation of our sin and then take specific action to align ourselves with His will.

Henry Blackaby

TODAY'S INTEGRITY BUILDER

If you're engaged in behavior that is displeasing to God, today is the day to stop. First, confess your sins to God. Then, ask Him what actions you should take in order to make things right again.

If we say, "We have no sin," we are deceiving ourselves, and the truth is not in us. If we confess our sins, He is faithful and righteous to forgive us our sins and to cleanse us from all unrighteousness.

1 John 1:8-9 Holman CSB

There will be more joy in heaven over one sinner who repents than over 99 righteous people who don't need repentance.

Luke 15:7 Holman CSB

But the Pharisees and their scribes were complaining to His disciples, "Why do you eat and drink with tax collectors and sinners?" Jesus replied to them, "The healthy don't need a doctor, but the sick do. I have not come to call the righteous, but sinners to repentance."

Luke 5:30-32 Holman CSB

TODAY'S PRAYER

When I stray from Your commandments, Lord, I must not only confess my sins, I must also turn from them. When I fall short, help me to change. When I reject Your Word and Your will for my life, guide me back to Your side. Forgive my sins, Dear Lord, and help me live according to Your plan for my life. Your plan is perfect, Father; I am not. Let me trust in You. Amen

ACCEPTING LIFE

Do not remember the past events, pay no attention to things
of old. Look, I am about to do something new;
even now it is coming. Do you not see it?
Indeed, I will make a way in the wilderness,
rivers in the desert.

Isaiah 43:18-19 Holman CSB

I f you're like most people, you like being in control. Period. You want things to happen according to your wishes and according to your timetable. But sometimes, God has other plans . . . and He always has the final word.

Oswald Chambers correctly observed, "Our Lord never asks us to decide for Him; He asks us to yield to Him—a very different matter." These words remind us that even when we cannot understand the workings of God, we must trust Him and accept His will.

All of us experience adversity and pain. As human beings with limited comprehension, we can never fully understand the will of our Father in heaven. But as believers in a benevolent God, we must always trust His providence.

When Jesus went to the Mount of Olives, as described in Luke 22, He poured out His heart to God. Jesus knew of the agony that He was destined to endure, but He also knew that God's will must be done. We, like our Savior, face trials that bring fear and trembling to the very depths of our souls, but like Christ, we too must ultimately seek God's will, not our own.

Are you embittered by a personal tragedy that you did not deserve and cannot understand? If so, it's time to make peace with life. It's time to forgive others, and, if necessary, to forgive yourself. It's time to accept the unchangeable past, to embrace the priceless present, and to have faith in the promise of tomorrow. It's time to trust God completely. And it's time to reclaim the peace—His peace—that can and should be yours.

I am truly grateful that faith enables me
to move past the question of "Why?"

—

Zig Ziglar

What cannot be altered must be borne, not blamed.

Thomas Fuller

Prayer may not get us what we want, but it will teach us to want what we need.

Vance Havner

The key to contentment is to consider. Consider who you are and be satisfied with that. Consider what you have and be satisfied with that. Consider what God's doing and be satisfied with that.

Luci Swindoll

Trust the past to God's mercy, the present to God's love, and the future to God's providence.

St. Augustine

Today's Integrity Builder

Acceptance means learning to trust God more. Today, think of at least one aspect of your life that you've been reluctant to accept, and then prayerfully ask God to help you trust Him more by accepting the past.

A man's heart plans his way, but the Lord determines his steps.

Proverbs 16:9 Holman CSB

For everything created by God is good, and nothing should be rejected if it is received with thanksgiving.

1 Timothy 4:4 Holman CSB

Should we accept only good from God and not adversity?

Job 2:10 Holman CSB

Come to terms with God and be at peace; in this way good will come to you.

Job 22:21 Holman CSB

Today's Prayer

Dear Lord, let me live in the present, not the past. Let me focus on my blessings, not my sorrows. Give me the wisdom to be thankful for the gifts that I do have, and not bitter about the things that I don't have. Let me accept what was, let me give thanks for what is, and let me have faith in what most surely will be: the promise of eternal life with You. Amen

THE RIGHT KIND OF ATTITUDE

A cheerful heart has a continual feast.

Proverbs 15:15 Holman CSB

O f course you've heard the saying, "Life is what you make it." And although that statement may seem very trite, it's also very true. You can choose a life filled to the brim with frustration and fear, or you can choose a life of abundance and peace. That choice is up to you—and only you—and it depends, to a surprising extent, upon your attitude.

What's your attitude today? Are you fearful, angry, bored, or worried? Are you pessimistic, perplexed, pained, and perturbed? Are you moping around with a frown on your face that's almost as big as the one in your heart? If so, God wants to have a little talk with you.

God created you in His own image, and He wants you to experience joy, contentment, peace, and abundance. But, God will not force you to experience these things; you must claim them for yourself.

God has given you free will, including the ability to influence the direction and the tone of your thoughts.

And, here's how God wants you to direct those thoughts:

Finally brothers, whatever is true, whatever is honorable, whatever is just, whatever is pure, whatever is lovely, whatever is commendable—if there is any moral excellence and if there is any praise—dwell on these things (Philippians 4:8 Holman CSB).

The quality of your attitude will help determine the quality of your life, so you must guard your thoughts accordingly. If you make up your mind to approach life with a healthy mixture of realism and optimism, you'll be rewarded. But, if you allow yourself to fall into the unfortunate habit of negative thinking, you will doom yourself to unhappiness, or mediocrity, or worse.

So, the next time you find yourself dwelling upon the negative aspects of your life, refocus your attention on things positive. The next time you find yourself falling prey to the blight of pessimism, stop yourself and turn your thoughts around. The next time you're tempted to waste valuable time gossiping or complaining, resist those temptations with all your might.

And remember this character-building tip: You'll never whine your way to the top . . . so don't waste your breath.

The people whom I have seen succeed best in life have always been cheerful and hopeful people who went about their business with a smile on their faces.

Charles Kingsley

Keep your feet on the ground, but let your heart soar as high as it will. Refuse to be average or to surrender to the chill of your spiritual environment.

A. W. Tozer

A positive attitude will have positive results because attitudes are contagious.

Zig Ziglar

The greater part of our happiness or misery depends on our dispositions, and not on our circumstances.

Martha Washington

Today's Integrity Builder

Today, create a positive attitude by focusing on opportunities, not roadblocks. Of course you may have experienced disappointments in the past, and you will undoubtedly experience some setbacks in the future. But don't invest large amounts of energy focusing on past misfortunes. Instead, look to the future with optimism and hope.

Make your own attitude that of Christ Jesus.

Philippians 2:5 Holman CSB

Finally brothers, whatever is true, whatever is honorable, whatever is just, whatever is pure, whatever is lovely, whatever is commendable—if there is any moral excellence and if there is any praise—dwell on these things.

Philippians 4:8 Holman CSB

For the word of God is living and powerful, and sharper than any two-edged sword, piercing even to the division of soul and spirit, and of joints and marrow, and is a discerner of the thoughts and intents of the heart.

Hebrews 4:12 NKJV

TODAY'S PRAYER

Lord, let me be an expectant Christian. Let me expect the best from You, and let me look for the best in others. If I become discouraged, Father, turn my thoughts and my prayers to You. Let me trust You, Lord, to direct my life. And, let me share my faith and optimism with others, today and every day that I live. Amen

DAY 99

A REGULAR DAILY DEVOTIONAL BUILDS CHARACTER

He awakens Me morning by morning,
He awakens My ear to hear as the learned.
The Lord God has opened My ear.

Isaiah 50:4-5 NKJV

Do you have a character-building, life-altering, standing appointment with God every morning? Is God your first priority, or do you talk with Him less frequently than that? If you're wise, you'll talk to God first thing every day, without exception.

Warren Wiersbe writes, "Surrender your mind to the Lord at the beginning of each day." And that's sound advice. When you begin each day with your head bowed and your heart lifted, you are reminded of God's love, His protection, and His commandments. Then, you can align your priorities for the coming day with the teachings and commandments that God has placed upon your heart.

Each day has 1,440 minutes—can you give God a few of them? Of course you can . . . and of course you should. So if you've acquired the unfortunate habit of trying to "squeeze" God into the corners of your life, it's time to reshuffle the items on your to-do list by placing God first. And if you haven't already done so, form the habit of spending quality time each morning with your Creator. He deserves it . . . and so, for that matter, do you.

A child of God should never
leave his bedroom in the morning
without being on good terms with God.

—

C. H. Spurgeon

We must appropriate the tender mercy of God every day after conversion or problems quickly develop. We need his grace daily in order to live a righteous life.

Jim Cymbala

A person with no devotional life generally struggles with faith and obedience.

Charles Stanley

I suggest you discipline yourself to spend time daily in a systematic reading of God's Word. Make this "quiet time" a priority that nobody can change.

Warren Wiersbe

Meditating upon His Word will inevitably bring peace of mind, strength of purpose, and power for living.

Bill Bright

TODAY'S INTEGRITY BUILDER

Get reacquainted with God every day. Would you like a foolproof formula for a better life? Here it is: stay in close contact with God. Hannah Whitall Smith wrote, "The crucial question for each of us is this: What do you think of Jesus, and do you yet have a personal acquaintance with Him?" Think about your relationship with Jesus: what it is and what it could be.

Lord, You are my lamp; the Lord illuminates my darkness.

2 Samuel 22:29 Holman CSB

Teach me Your way, Lord, and I will live by Your truth. Give me an undivided mind to fear Your name.

Psalm 86:11 Holman CSB

I will instruct you and show you the way to go; with My eye on you, I will give counsel.

Psalm 32:8 Holman CSB

Happy is the man who finds wisdom, and the man who gains understanding.

Proverbs 3:13 NKJV

TODAY'S PRAYER

Lord, help me to hear Your direction for my life in the quiet moments when I study Your Holy Word. And as I go about my daily activities, let everything that I say and do be pleasing to You. Amen

FOR GOD SO LOVED THE WORLD

For God loved the world in this way:
He gave His only Son, so that everyone who believes in Him
will not perish but have eternal life.

John 3:16 Holman CSB

Christ sacrificed His life on the cross so that we might have eternal life. This gift, freely given by God's only begotten Son, is the priceless possession of everyone who accepts Him as Lord and Savior. God is waiting patiently for each of us to accept the gift of eternal life. Let us claim Christ's gift today.

God's grace is not earned . . . thank goodness! To earn God's love and His gift of eternal life would be far beyond the abilities of even the most righteous man or woman. Thankfully, grace is not an earthly reward for righteous behavior; it is a blessed spiritual gift which can be accepted by believers who dedicate themselves to God through Christ. When we accept Christ into our hearts, we are saved by His grace.

God's grace is the ultimate gift, and we owe to Him the ultimate in thanksgiving. Let us praise the Creator for

His priceless gift, and let us share the Good News with all who cross our paths. We return our Father's love by accepting His grace and by sharing His message and His love. When we do, we are eternally blessed . . . and the hosts of heaven rejoice!

The way to be saved is not to delay,
but to come and take.

—

D. L. Moody

God did everything necessary to provide for our forgiveness by sacrificing His perfect, holy Son as the atoning substitute for our sins.

Franklin Graham

We had better quickly discover whether we have mere religion or a real experience with Jesus, whether we have outward observance of religious forms or hearts that beat in tune with God.

Jim Cymbala

To lose us was too great a pain for God to bear, and so he took it upon himself to rescue us. The Son of God came "to give his life as a ransom for many" (Matt. 20:28).

John Eldredge

The essence of salvation is an about-face from self-centeredness to God-centeredness.

Henry Blackaby

TODAY'S INTEGRITY BUILDER

The time is now. If you have already welcomed Christ into your heart as your personal Savior, then you are safe. If you're still sitting on the fence, the time to accept Him is this very moment.

And we have seen and we testify that the Father has sent the Son as Savior of the world.

1 John 4:14 Holman CSB

Blessed be the God and Father of our Lord Jesus Christ. According to His great mercy, He has given us a new birth into a living hope through the resurrection of Jesus Christ from the dead.

1 Peter 1:3 Holman CSB

This saying is trustworthy and deserving of full acceptance: "Christ Jesus came into the world to save sinners."

1 Timothy 1:15 Holman CSB

The sun will be turned to darkness, and the moon to blood, before the great and remarkable day of the Lord comes; then whoever calls on the name of the Lord will be saved.

Acts 2:20-21 Holman CSB

TODAY'S PRAYER

Dear Lord, I am only here on this earth for a brief while. But, You have offered me the priceless gift of eternal life through Your Son Jesus. I accept Your gift, Lord, with thanksgiving and praise. Let me share the Good News of my salvation with all those who need Your healing touch. Amen

He stores up success for the upright;
He is a shield for those who live with integrity.

—

Proverbs 2:7 Holman CSB